The Greatest Power Within You

A Journalist's View by Arline Phillips-Han

ARLINE PHILLIPS-HAN

WESTBOW PRESS®
A DIVISION OF THOMAS NELSON & ZONDERVAN

WestBow Press books may be ordered through booksellers or by contacting:

WestBow Press
A Division of Thomas Nelson & Zondervan
1663 Liberty Drive
Bloomington, IN 47403
www.westbowpress.com
1 (866) 928-1240

Scriptures cited in this book are from The New King James Version unless otherwise indicated, such as Scriptures from The New International Version (NIV)

ISBN: 978-1-9736-8068-0 (sc)
ISBN: 978-1-9736-8069-7 (hc)
ISBN: 978-1-9736-8070-3 (e)

Library of Congress Control Number: 2019919504

Print information available on the last page.

WestBow Press rev. date: 12/05/2019

CONTENTS

PREFACE

When my life was shattered by a series of events that left me unable to see anything outside the dark shadows, and unable to go on as a happy, productive person, I turned to the only readily available source of help that I knew about. I sat on my living room sofa and prayed that God the Holy Spirit would help me want to live. He lived up to His reputation as "the Helper and Comforter" sent by God the Father to indwell the hearts of believers. The presence of the Holy Spirit within me is the power that transformed me and stays with me.

For every person who knows what it is like to live with a broken heart or a broken spirit due to disabling disease or injury, or with a child who is suffering, this book is for you. I felt compelled to write it in order to bring to fresh memory the scriptures that define the many roles that the Holy Spirit plays in human life. The book captures the highlights of extensive Bible study, which explains why I am no longer splintered and beaten, but a whole person realizing His purposes for me.

I begin with the Bible's account of the resurrection of Jesus Christ from the grave after the most brutal Roman Crucifixion: the focal event of the 1965 American epic film, *The Greatest Story Ever Told.* The Bible attributes the resurrection to the power of the Holy Spirit; upon that foundation, it explains how that same power changed the hearts and souls of Christ's first disciples. The courageous ministry of these common working-class men, in the face of life-threatening obstacles, established the faith (my chosen faith) known as Christianity.

Through this book, I invite you to follow some of the trailblazers from Galilee and Tarsus, who heeded Christ's teaching to ***"walk in the Spirit"*** and became the valiant ambassadors whose ministry generated cultural advancements in most of the world as we know it today. The power that invaded their hearts inaugurated a new worldview based on a New Covenant relationship between us and God, replacing desperation and fear with new vision and hope.

The pioneer missionaries became the best definitions of life led by the Spirit, outstripping biblical comparisons to savage wind and purifying fire. The wind and fire that were experienced by praying believers on the day of Pentecost two thousand years ago were mere symbols of God's incredible power to invade the hearts of Christ's disciples and to do the same for all who believe in Him and choose to live for Him. Assurance of that fact is provided in His promise in John 3:16: "For God so loved the world that He gave His only begotten Son that whoever believes in Him will not perish, but have everlasting life."

I present God the Son (Jesus) and God the Holy Spirit in the context of the scriptures, which introduce both of them as coequal with God the Father. In this framework, we see the spectacular work of the three holy and omniscient Persons Who comprise one God, Who created and sustains all living things.

This book is an incomplete treatise on how God's gift of the Holy Spirit impacts the lives of believers, especially on how He transformed my own life when I most needed spiritual rescue.

The blessing of the Spirit living in me is the greatest story about my life. He gave me a new heart of understanding and commitment, and a new vision of the kind of Christian I can be with His presence within. He opened my eyes to new possibilities for making a difference in the lives of others who need Him as I need Him. The good news for all believers is that, simply for the asking, He can be *your* source of the greatest power that can inhabit the human heart.

Arline Phillips-Han

CHAPTER 1

JESUS LOST AND FOUND

The sun was yet to break through the haze over the garden estate of Joseph of Arimathea, outside the city gates of Jerusalem. Dark shadows obscured the limestone tomb that would become known historically as the place where Jesus Christ was buried and resurrected three days later in the month of April two thousand years ago.

The garden was quiet in the misty darkness just before dawn, until soft footsteps were heard in the direction of the tomb. As the story is told in the Gospels of Matthew, Mark, Luke, and John, three women walked past the tawny stone walls, carrying sweet burial spices and fragrant oils to use in anointing the body of Christ. The women had watched His Crucifixion on a rugged Roman cross by the cruelest method known in that day. His mother, Mary, who was there to see her beloved son slain, had been taken home by the apostle John, who would care for her for the rest of her life at the request of Jesus Himself.

Jesus had been humiliated and rejected by Jewish leaders in the nation of Israel but was given a dignified burial in a new tomb donated by Joseph, a wealthy and noble member of the Sanhedrin, the Jewish council. As a matter of historical record, there are no conflicting traditions regarding Jesus's burial. Joseph believed He was the Son of God but kept his faith secret for fear of losing his membership in the synagogue. By donating the tomb, which he had hewn out of the rocks of his garden, he threw in his lot with the party of Jesus and lost his standing with the ruling caste.

Two of the women, Mary Magdalene and Mary the mother of James, had stood next to the tomb while Joseph and Nicodemus, a Jewish religious leader, wrapped Jesus's body in layer upon layer of fine linen saturated with seventy-five pounds of embalming spices. Now they walked to the gravesite with other women, fretting about who might roll away the heavy stone with the attached seal of the Roman governor closing the opening to the sepulcher. The governor's seal could only be broken on penalty of death, yet the women were determined to open the tomb.

To their shock, they arrived to find the stone had been moved away. There are variations in the four Gospel accounts of the Crucifixion and burial, as would occur in the news reports of four different journalists. The most detailed eyewitness report comes from Matthew, the former Roman tax collector who left his regional customs office in Capernaum at the northeast end of the Sea of Galilee to follow Jesus.

"Behold, there was a great earthquake, for an angel of the Lord descended from heaven and came and rolled back the stone from the door, and sat on it," Matthew wrote in the book that bears his name. "His countenance was like lightning, and his clothing was white as snow. And the guards shook for fear of him and became like dead men" (Matthew 28:2–4).

Matthew continued, "The angel said to the women, 'Do not be afraid, for I know that you seek Jesus who was crucified. He is not here; for He is risen as He said. Come, see the place where the Lord lay. And go quickly and tell His disciples that He is risen from the dead, and indeed He is going before you into Galilee; there you will see Him.'"

The women, stunned and fearful, rushed to tell the disciples. On the way, they ran into Jesus alive and walking.

"Rejoice!" He called out. They ran to hold Him by the feet and worshipped Him.

"Do not be afraid. Go and tell My brethren to go to Galilee and there they will see Me," He said (Matthew 28:10).

Hearing Him speak so confidently, as He had always spoken, seeing him, and touching Him, the women knew He had conquered death. He had been dead; now they saw Him alive. As they tried to grasp the enormity of that fact, their hearts were filled with joy that overcame fear.

At the entrance to the tomb, the Roman guards, who had fainted when they saw the radiant angels, regained their senses and wasted no time in taking action. Their lives depended on letting Jewish authorities know they had not slept or let down their guard at any point. They rushed to report to the high priests in Jerusalem, who were apparently panic-stricken to hear the body of the rabble-rousing preacher was missing. The priests called the elders to meet with the guards and offered them a large sum of money to spread a rumor that the disciples had stolen the body while they slept. The elders assured the guards, "If this reaches the governor's ears, we will appease him and make you secure."

The guards accepted the bribe and scattered in different directions to spread the lie as instructed. If the corpse was actually stolen, logic would say it would eventually be found and abruptly end faith in Jesus as the long-awaited Messiah or Savior. His Hebrew name, Yeshua, means "Yahweh (the Lord) is salvation," which is exactly what He claimed to bring to humankind. But of course, no rational person would worship a dead religious leader.

Jewish leaders were serious in their search for Jesus's body, but no corpse fitting His description was found at that time or since. If He had been found alive and talking normally, His resurrection would not be a wild and speculative idea; He would be seen and heard.

> Angels, defined in scripture as God's messengers and agents of comfort, appeared at momentous times throughout Jesus's earthly life, from His conception and birth to His baptism, in His beseeching prayer to His Father in the Garden of Gethsemane, and in His resurrection. In regard to the resurrection, the question is whether there was one angel at the gravesite, as Matthew and Mark reported, or two angels, as Luke and John described. The discrepancy is puzzling, yet the four gospels share similar accounts of Jesus's arrest, execution, burial, and resurrection, written in different styles and focused on different aspects of the events.

At the time of the Crucifixion, the guards would have been among the few people, along with the mourners, who were close to the cross where they could witness some of the supernatural events described by Matthew: darkness over the land from noon until 3 p.m. (note the scripture is that specific); the top-to-bottom ripping of the thick woven temple veil, which separated worshippers in the temple from the ark of the covenant; an earthquake splitting the rocks; graves opening and long-departed saints rising up and walking the streets of Jerusalem. Qualified secular historians have confirmed the time frame in which darkness hovered over the land during the mid-afternoon hours of the Crucifixion.

The centurion (commander of a hundred soldiers) on guard at the cross and his retinue of soldiers, hardened men accustomed to executing criminals, heard Jesus cry out, ***"Eli, Eli, lama sabachthani?" (My God, My God, why have you forsaken Me?).*** He died at about 3 p.m. on the Day of Preparation, the day before the Sabbath would begin at sunset. The sentinel soldiers felt the ground shake and were heard to say, "Truly this was the Son of God" (Matthew 27:54).

Mystery Shrouds the Garden and the City of Jerusalem

Incredible events surrounded the empty tomb. As the apostle John wrote in his Gospel account, Mary Magdalene went to the tomb early, while it was still dark, on the first day of the week and saw that the stone had been removed from the opening. She ran and found Peter and the other disciple whom Jesus loved (referring to himself), saying to them, "They have taken away the Lord out of the tomb, and we do not know where they have laid Him" (John 20:1–2).

Peter and John ran to look for themselves. John outran Peter and stooped to peer into the tomb where he saw the linen graveclothes lying there, but no corpse. Peter ran all the way inside the open sepulcher, and he too saw the linen clothes lying there and the handkerchief that had wrapped Jesus's head folded together in a place by itself (Matthew 20:4–7). When John followed Peter by walking inside the tomb, he too saw the handkerchief folded and placed separately. He declared that what he saw cemented his belief. Writing in third person, he said, "Then the other disciple, who came to the tomb first, went in also and he saw and believed" (John 20:8).

Now the mystery of who moved the stone (the title of a 1930s classic apologetic by Frank Morison) was compounded by the mystery of who folded the cloth that had wrapped Jesus's head. Of course, logic would suggest it had to be Jesus Himself. The greater mystery is how He could rise to His feet after lying dead in the tomb for three days, wrapped in spice-laden graveclothes, and walk out of a heavily blocked stone sepulcher past the stoutly armed Roman soldiers standing guard?

The question of how the resurrection could have happened is an historically pivotal one. The answer is not a blind leap of faith, as many skeptics claim. Christ Himself addresses the question in a powerful statement quoted in John 10:17–18: ***"Therefore does my Father love me, because I lay down my life, that I might take it up again. No man taketh it from me, but I lay it down to take it up again."***

A few facts are verified in secular history books as well as the Bible: He was proven dead by a variety of sources at the scene at the time of the resurrection and was seen alive for forty days after resurrection by all of His original disciples and by at least five hundred people who saw Him in one place at the same time (see 1 Corinthians 15:3–8). Many renowned Bible scholars today say these and other facts support the resurrection of Jesus as a historical event and explain why He dramatically changed the course of history.

The disciples went home after their first close look inside the empty tomb. But Mary Magdalene stayed at the scene crying. As she wept, she looked into the tomb and saw two angels, one at the head and the other at the foot of the place where Jesus's body had lain. The angels asked why she was weeping, and she said, "Because they have taken away my Lord, and I do not know where they have laid Him."

Mary turned and saw a man she mistook for the gardener, not suspecting it could be Jesus.

"Woman, why are you weeping? Who are you seeking?" Jesus asked.

Mary said, "Sir, if you have carried Him away, tell me where you have laid Him, and I will take Him away" (John 20:15). Then she heard His familiar voice calling, ***"Mary!"***

"*Rabonni!* (Teacher)," she replied in Aramaic. Jesus had cleansed her of seven demons and transformed her life. Her heart was devoted to Him, and she had become a close follower. The Gospel of Luke lists her among the women who traveled with Jesus and helped support His ministry (Luke 8:2–3).

"Do not cling to Me, for I have not yet ascended to My Father," He said to Mary. ***"Go to My brethren and say to them, 'I am ascending to My father and your Father, and to My God and your God"*** (John 20:17).

It was a climactic moment. She was standing outside the sepulcher on that morning after Passover Sabbath, and was there when He took His first steps outside the grave. As the sun was rising, she was first to see the event that would change human understanding of life and death. When He conquered death, He demonstrated the reality of His Father's promise of eternal life for all who believe in Him (John 3:16).

Alfred Edersheim, the British scholar who wrote the esteemed book, *The Life and Times of Jesus the Messiah,* first published in the 1880s, concluded in his chapter on the resurrection, "The importance of all this cannot be adequately expressed in words. A dead Christ might have been a Teacher and Wonder-worker, and remembered and loved as such. But only a risen and living Christ could be the Savior, the Life and the Life-Giver—and, as such, preached to all men. And of this most blessed truth we have the fullest and most unquestionable evidence."

The women who came to the tomb reported that the angels at the scene urged them to recall what Jesus had said about Himself while still in Galilee: ***"The Son of Man must be delivered into the hands of sinful men and be crucified, and the third day rise again."*** They had no problem remembering Jesus saying this. As they pieced together everything that had happened, they realized He had predicted His own death on the cross and His resurrection within three days. They were sure He had returned to life because they saw Him and talked to Him.

What brought Him to the point of being targeted for murder stemmed from Judaism's rock-hard resistance to any religious faith outside their own. For centuries, the Jews had worshipped a singular, sovereign God. They rejected the idea of God taking on human flesh and thus had no rationale for believing there could be a Son of God. And here, at the world center of their religious practice, there had appeared this young man claiming to be God's Son sent to earth to save people from penalties deserved for sins that ruin relationships with God the Father.

At the time Jesus began His ministry in the Galilean countryside, there was no room for a new religious faith, especially a radical call to love one's enemies while also giving supreme love to God and neighbor. Jesus taught a new ideology that extended fellowship and mercy beyond their restricted boundaries and violated Jewish scruples about the law, including some of their stringent Sabbath Day rules. He asserted a lot of authority for Himself, including the ability to forgive people of their sins, which they knew was a prerogative of God the Father.

The priests, elders, and scribes of Judaism, who did not believe Jesus was God, were staunch guardians of their ancient religion and proud of their synagogue positions that brought them financial and social status. The Torah (first five books of the Bible) was their guidebook. They were serious in daily religious practice, honoring the laws of Moses, and they wanted nothing to disturb their traditional way of life.

Above all the factors that provoked their hatred of Jesus was His stupendous claim to be the Christ, the Son of God and equal with Him. He stated without qualification, ***"I am the way, the truth and the life. No one comes to the Father except through Me"*** (John 14:6).

When global evangelist Billy Graham (1918–2018) first read this claim while he was a young student, he said he had to wrestle with this question: Was Jesus who He claimed to be, or was He the biggest liar, fraud, and charlatan in history? He decided on the basis of scripture that Jesus is the Son of God. Actually, every person confronts the same question and will decide whether to believe it or dismiss it.

One Sabbath Day when Jesus spoke at his hometown synagogue in Nazareth, He read a prophecy from Isaiah which He claimed was the mission God sent <u>Him</u> to carry out:

"The Spirit of the Lord God is upon Me, because the Lord has anointed Me to preach good tidings to the poor;

He has sent me to heal the brokenhearted, to proclaim liberty to the captives **[freedom from the bondage of sin]** ***and recovery of sight to the blind, to proclaim liberty to the captives, and the opening of the prison to those who are bound; to proclaim the acceptable year of the Lord and the day of vengeance of our God; to comfort all who mourn, to console those who mourn in Zion, to give them beauty for ashes, the oil of joy for mourning, the garment of praise for the spirit of heaviness, that they may be called trees of righteousness, the planting of the Lord, that He may be glorified"*** (Isaiah 61:1–3).

Jesus closed the book of prophecy, handed it to the minister, and sat down. With all eyes fastened on Him, He stated that He was the one anointed by His Father God to fulfill this prophecy, which Isaiah had proclaimed seven hundred years earlier. He knew He was sent to announce the good news: the transformation of a person who repents his or her sin to serve God and in whom God implants a new heart.

Worshipers in the synagogue that day were furious that Jesus would assume such authority; they rose from their seats and chased Him out, intending to throw Him headfirst from a steep cliff at the edge of town. But He slipped away and left Nazareth for the fishing village of Capernaum, where He continued teaching and caring for the people as the Holy Spirit led Him.

As He identified Himself with the Father in a manner that sounded frankly preposterous, the Jewish authorities accused Him of being a false king, a false prophet, and a false Messiah (Matthew 26:57–68; Mark 14:53–65; Luke 22:66–71).

Jesus could do nothing good in the eyes of Judaism's hierarchy, who viewed his accomplishments as threats to the strength and the future of Judaism. He not only angered them by healing victims of leprosy, paralysis, fever, blindness, bleeding disorders, and demon possession, but even more so by healing some sufferers, such as the man with a withered hand and the woman possessed by an evil spirit, on the Sabbath Day, a violation of Jewish law. They ridiculed the miracle worker, who was attracting a legion of followers.

So many cures, hour by hour and day after day, until adversarial Pharisees accused Jesus of casting out devils by the ruler of the demons (Matthew 9:34). He became so popular that Mark wrote in his Gospel, "Jesus could no longer enter the city [speaking of Capernaum], but was outside in deserted places, and they came to Him from every direction."

He was selflessly attentive to the people, but He also showed a ferocious response to disrespect for His Father. During the Passover celebration, He caught sight of money-changers cheating worshippers in the temple's outer courtyard for the Gentiles. Men were profiting at the expense of the poor, and He would not stand by and watch the injustice. Jesus moved in angrily. He made a whip of cords and drove out those who were corrupting His Father's house, along with their inventory of bulls, sheep, goats, doves, and pigeons prepared for sacrifice.

He actually exposed exploitation at the temple, where the chief priests and Pharisees were leading the world assembly of Jewish worshippers. He overturned the money tables, sending silver and bronze coins clattering across the pavement. Money-changers and vendors raced down the courtyard steps, sheep and cattle grunted and moaned in a rowdy stampede, and feathers flew from slatted crates.

Immediately after He unleashed fury on the people desecrating the temple courtyard, a group of children saw Him praying and healing sick and disabled people who had gathered there. The excited youngsters ran up to Him, shouting, "Hosanna to the Son of David!" (referring to Jesus's ancestral ties to Israeli King David).

The destructive episode, certainly costly to those profiting from the sale of sacrificial animals, infuriated Jewish authorities. They now saw Him as a dangerous revolutionary, and they would stop at nothing to destroy Him. From this day, He was virtually on death row.

No Ordinary Galilean Carrying out His Father's Will

To look at Jesus was to see a typical young Galilean man, most likely a rugged outdoorsman in sturdy robe and well-worn leather sandals, but to track him in real time was to see a man on the move, living with purpose in the moments. As the New Testament Gospel writers describe His life, He devoted a little over three years to preaching God's kingdom come to earth and His plan for saving people from sin. He surprised the people with an almost constant stream of healings, expulsion of demons or tormenting spirits, and at least three publicly witnessed resurrections from the dead. He spent many days in the synagogue, on the cobblestone streets, and on dusty byroads, informing men and women that this world is not all there is, there is a vastly superior way. He worked as if time itself was running out.

He drew aggressive opposition from the first day He announced the Kingdom of God was at hand, a kingdom not of this earth and greater than the vast Roman Empire. He compared this kingdom to a treasure hidden in a field, so precious that if people stumble upon it, they will give everything they own to possess it. More than that, a kingdom that will bring relief and hope to the poorest people in society, a new way, through Himself, to save men and women from sin and help them live with greater joy now and enjoy the reward of eternal life.

Eternal Life: God's Phenomenal Promise Begins Here and Now

The concept of eternal life is presented in Matthew, Mark, and Luke as an ultimate reward not to begin until after death, but the apostle John describes eternal life as both a futuristic and present-day reality for all who believe in Christ as Lord and Savior. John, who was an eyewitness to the entire earthly life of Christ, emphasized eternal life and the divinity of Christ throughout his Gospel.

"God has given us eternal life, and this life is in His Son. Whoever has the Son has life; whoever does not have the Son of God does not have life" (1 John 5:11–12).

Jesus clearly states His own thoughts on the subject in a prayer at the end of his final address to the disciples (and to all future believers): ***"Father the hour has come. Glorify your Son, that Your Son also may glorify You. As you have given Him authority over all flesh, that He should give eternal life to as many as You have given Him, and this is eternal life, that they may know You, the only true God, and Jesus Christ, whom you have sent"*** (John 17:1–4).

Jesus under Constant Probe and Threats by Religious Leaders

The more Jesus healed the sick and shared His wisdom, the more He was targeted by Jewish leaders. They shadowed Him, looking for any chance He might say or do something threatening to Roman rule. They set traps with their questions: Did He honor Caesar? (Yes, and He told others to give to Caesar what was due him.) Did he flout the Jewish religious laws? (Yes.) Did He actually forgive people of their sins, which only God can do? (Yes.) Did He ignore Jewish Sabbath laws by healing the sick on that holy day? (Yes, many times.) Did He dine and socialize with taxpayers and other lowlifes? (Yes.)

And did He honor His obligation to pay his taxes? A group of Pharisees buttonholed Jesus and asked, "What do you think: is it lawful to pay taxes to Caesar or not?"

Jesus escaped the trap of a yes-or-no question and asked them to show Him the tax money. They brought him a denarius, one of the standard Roman coins used to pay taxes, and He asked, ***"Whose image and inscription is this?"***

They answered, "Caesar's."

"Render therefor to Caesar the things that are Caesar's and to God the things that are God's," He said (Matthew 22:21). The Pharisees were unable to refute his response and left in amazement.

Finally, although Jesus had not broken any Roman laws, they decided that His claim to be the Son of God and One with God was blasphemous against Rome and therefore a crime for which He should be killed. They conspired how to arrest Him by stealth. "We have a law, and by our law He ought to die because He made himself the Son of God," they said. (John 19:7). They had already stoned to death many God-anointed prophets; one more would be no sweat.

While they plotted His murder, He continued to perform miracles that stopped people in their tracks and gave rise to tough questions: What was driving Him? Was God actually in the miracles?

In the eyes of Israeli Jews, He was the son of a carpenter raised in a peasant village by a young Jewish couple seen frequently in the synagogue. But Jesus was not necessarily a peasant. He grew up in Nazareth at a time when it was closely connected to the sophisticated Greco-Roman village of Sepphoris, known as the jewel of the Galilee and popular site of silk trade and construction industry. In Sepphoris, He probably rubbed shoulders with wealthy pro-Roman Jews, Greeks, and various travelers from as far west as Egypt and as far to the east as Persia and India. Ruins of the village can be seen on a hill in western Galilee.

In the heyday of His brief earthly ministry, He became known for much more than the feats that drew public attention, such as walking on water, changing water into wine at a wedding, and stopping a storm at sea with a command. The resurrections He performed cemented Him in the public consciousness as God-like, if not actually God. Scripture underscores the latter description; His declaration of Himself as the only begotten Son of God is a statement for people of all time to grapple with.

Many people in the village of Bethany knew firsthand about His unforgettable miracle of raising Lazarus from the dead, an accomplishment that further enraged Jewish authorities and fueled their desire to kill Him. Who could compare with a self-described Son of God, Who raised a dead man to life four days after his burial? They had never heard of anything like it.

No one at that time and place had a clue as to what empowered Him to restore life to the dead. The Gospels relate amazing detail. Jesus was thirty years old and preparing to preach publicly when He sought His cousin John and found him in Perea on the Jordanian side of the Jordan River, baptizing converts who had responded to his urgent message, "Repent, for the Kingdom of God is at hand." Jesus asked to be among the people undergoing baptism.

John, who became known as John the Baptist, saw Jesus coming and said to the crowd at the riverbank, "Behold! The lamb of God who takes away the sin of the world. This is He, of whom I said, 'After me comes a Man who is preferred before me, for He was before me" (John 1:29–30). He had also said, "I indeed baptize you with water unto repentance, but He who is coming after me is mightier than I, whose sandals I am not worthy to carry. He will baptize you with the Holy Spirit and fire" (Matthew 3:11).

In scripture, fire is a commonly used metaphor for God and His judgment (Isaiah 66:16).

Jesus asked to be baptized, but John at first refused, saying Jesus should be baptizing him. But he followed through when Jesus insisted that He needed to go through this traditional purification ritual, ***"to fulfill all righteousness."***

Mark describes the scene of Jesus being baptized in the Jordan River: "And immediately, coming up from the water, He saw the heavens parting and the [Holy] Spirit descending like a dove and lighting upon Him. Then a voice came from heaven, ***'You are my beloved Son in whom I am well pleased.'"*** The scripture in this case involves God the Son undergoing baptism, the blessing of

God the Holy Spirit in the visible form of a dove, and God the Father audibly praising His Son, Jesus.

Shortly after the baptism, the Holy Spirit led Jesus into the harsh, dry Judean wilderness, where He spent forty days and forty nights, fasting and praying. In the desert, Satan tempted Him to give up the idea of ministry in exchange for wealth, power, fame, or all the above. At a point when He was weak from going days without food, the devil tempted Him to turn stones into bread. But He tersely dismissed the tempter: ***"Away with you, Satan! For it is written, 'You shall worship the Lord your God, and Him only you shall serve'"*** (Matthew 4:10).

In the midst of the devil's temptations, Jesus said, ***"It is written, Man shall not live by bread alone, but by every word that comes from the mouth of God.... It is also written, You shall not put the Lord your God to the test."*** The devil left, and angels came to attend to Him. He returned to Galilee in the power of the Spirit, and news about Him spread through the area.

Author's Reflection: Eternal Life in the Here and Now

Because Jesus Christ is alive, as the Bible documents and many historians support, I needed to decide whether to believe He is who He claimed to be, and follow Him, or shrug Him off. From early childhood, I decided to believe in Jesus, although I understood very little in my early years. I can't think of a time when I would have shrugged Him off, but if I had done so in the interest of living my life on my own terms, I would have simply postponed the need to answer the greatest questions of human existence.

Naturally, the important questions did not come to my mind until after years of Bible study. Now the questions seem urgent in light of the obvious limitations of life. The questions flit through my mind virtually every day: Does my life have worthwhile purpose now and in the long term? What does God think of my life? Will I know anything personally about life after death?

During times of profound emotional pain, which brought me to my knees, I repeatedly asked myself whether this is all I can reasonably expect from life. I've been searching the Bible, and I now know there is a great deal more. As I write this, deeper insights are reaching me through the Holy Spirit. The Bible has a lot to say to help us answer the questions.

One of my least expected discoveries, made while studying scriptures regarding the life of Christ, is that eternal life begins in the here and now for every person who believes in Him as their Lord and Savior. There is no waiting time between my decision (or yours) and the fact we are already living everlasting life with His Spirit alive in our hearts (see John 3:36).

Are we talking about an impossible dream, or the greatest miracle of all time? I think it is this discovery that saves a troubled soul, even mine, and makes life a journey of hope and joy in this present day.

CHAPTER 2

JESUS RAISES A FRIEND NAMED LAZARUS FROM DEATH TO LIFE

The actions of Jesus positively changed or saved the lives of every person He touched, in some cases healing many people at the same time. His miraculous raising of Lazarus to life after his burial in a rock-sealed cave occurred in Bethany, less than two miles from Jerusalem, six days before the Passover. Lazarus had been dead for four days, a full day after his soul would have left his body, according to Jewish belief at that time.

The Gospel of John points out that Lazarus was one of Jesus's closest friends and that He wept for him before walking to the cave and calling out, ***"Lazarus, come forth!"***

Lazarus walked out of the tomb stiff-legged like a mummy in layered strips of linen; he had to be unwrapped from head to toe.

"Loose him and let him go," Jesus said (John 11:44).

Spectacular as it was to see Lazarus free of his graveclothes and walking the village roads, the moment was far more historic in demonstrating that Jesus harbored life within Himself and was the giver of life. His actions supported His claim, ***"I am the way, the truth, and the life."*** Chief priests plotted how they might kill Lazarus after seeing that his resurgence of life after death prompted many Jews to believe in Jesus. The Bible is silent on the outcome of this plot.

As soon as the miracle became widely known to enemies of Christ, who would not stand for His growing popularity, it was His own death sentence. No other existing religious faith was known to have raised the dead to life.

Before calling Lazarus out of the tomb, Jesus comforted his grieving sister, Martha. In words that have consoled millions of believers since that day, He said, ***"I am the resurrection and the life. He who believes in Me, though he may die, he shall live. And whoever lives and believes in Me shall never die"*** (John 11:25). In His own words, Christ claimed that He is a virtual fountain of eternal life and that He promises eternal life to all believers.

Many people came to visit Lazarus, along with his sisters Mary and Martha, at their home in Bethany near the Mount of Olives. But despite talking with him and hearing the eyewitness accounts of his sisters and others, critics debated the feasibility of the event. The elite Sadducees, proud landowners and aristocrats who did not believe in the possibility of life after death, declared it did not happen. The Pharisees, fervent Jewish nationalists who strictly obeyed the law of Moses and believed in the resurrection of life, decided the reports of Lazarus were too threatening to ignore. Both opposing parties of Judaism (the Sadducees and the Pharisees) realized resurrections of the dead would attract a great following.

The noted French theologian and reformer John Calvin (1509–1564) said of this event, "Not only did Christ give a remarkable proof of His divine power in Lazarus, but He likewise placed before our eyes a lively image of our future resurrection." Theologians Francis

Moloney and Daniel Harrington viewed the raising of Lazarus from death to life as a "pivotal miracle" that started the chain of events leading to Christ's Crucifixion and resurrection.

Sadducees and Pharisees were there to see the formerly dead Lazarus talking to friends in town and at a dinner hosted by Martha. Many of the local folk knew who called Lazarus out of the grave and courageously declared their belief in Him. Others believed, but dared not say so, and some made no effort to hide their disgust. People recalled two earlier times when Jesus raised the dead to life: the twelve-year-old daughter of Rabbi Jairus in Capernaum and the widow's son, who was being carried to a cemetery in the town of Nain.

Jewish leaders became more fearful as hundreds of residents in the greater Jerusalem area began to follow Jesus Christ. They tightened their plots to kill Him, so that wherever He went, the threat of execution loomed over His head (John 11:8 and 16). Scripture is unclear about what happened to Lazarus after he was restored to life. How long did he live before he died again? The Bible does not answer this question but does make clear that Jesus remained alive after His resurrection; He did not go to His grave but was seen by many people at the time He was lifted up from the earth in living bodily form. His apostles were standing next to Him when He left.

In response to the Lazarus miracle, the chief priests and Pharisees called a meeting of the Sanhedrin to determine what should be done with Jesus. They said to one another, "If we let Him alone like this, everyone will believe in Him, and the Romans will come and take away both our place and nation" (John 11:47–48). They had a self-serving motive for wanting Him dead: self-preservation.

Caiaphas, who was chief priest that year, said to the priests and Pharisees, "You know nothing at all. Nor do you consider that it is expedient for us that one man should die for the people, and not that the whole nation should perish." (He predicted Jesus would die for the nation.)

Dark Night of the Soul for Disciple Named Judas

One tragic footnote to Christ's life was a man named Judas, from the small town of Kerioth in south Judea, one of the twelve disciples He originally chose to follow Him. Judas was an honorable name until he betrayed Jesus to Jerusalem authorities while they were on their way to arrest Him in the dark of night.

As treasurer for the disciples, Judas carried the moneybag and was known to skim funds for himself (John 12:6) At the Passover meal (Last Supper) hosted by Jesus in Jerusalem, at a moment unexpected by everyone there except Jesus, he slipped out of the room and into the night. He went to see the chief priests and asked what they might pay him if he helped the Sanhedrin find Jesus in a secret place to arrest Him. The priests gave Judas thirty pieces of silver, enough to send him running to inform the soldiers.

Jesus knew what Judas was up to; He had predicted at the supper that someone at the table would betray Him. After the meal ended, early in the evening, He walked to the Garden of Gethsemane. In the shadows of the olive trees, aware of the torture He would face at the hands of Roman soldiers, He prayed in anguish, ***"Father, if it is your will, take this cup away from me; nevertheless, not my will but yours be done."*** As He prayed, He sweat blood, which is a real, but rare medical problem called hematidrosis, usually occurring during extreme stress. He knew that when He took upon Himself the full weight of human sin, He would be temporarily separated from His Father, Who could not look upon sin. His anxiety was profound, and at this terrible time, an angel came to comfort Him.

When darkness fell that night, Judas walked into the garden, leading an armed posse of temple guards carrying lighted torches. He approached Jesus with open arms and kissed Him, signaling to the guards, who drew their swords. At some point, when he realized Jesus had been sentenced to death, he was gripped by remorse. He went into the temple, threw the silver coins on the floor, and confessed to the chief priests and elders, "I have sinned in that I have betrayed innocent blood."

But the authorities rebuffed Judas, saying, "What's that to us?"

Judas obviously regretted his betrayal of Jesus but did not ask Him for forgiveness. Before that night was over, he ended his life by hanging himself (Matthew 27:5). His motives remain unclear, but his betrayal of Jesus to the Roman guards indicate he had no clue as to Who Jesus is, or did not believe He was the Son of God. While Matthew reports Judas went away and hung himself, Luke's Gospel says he fell into a field and that his body ruptured and his bowels spilled out. Some Bible commentators have suggested both could have occurred, that he may have hung himself from a tree and fallen onto the field after his body decayed and bloated.

The biblical accounts concur that Judas killed himself. His name became synonymous with traitor. Even more tragically for Jesus was the fact that all His disciples, except John, forsook Him and fled from the scene (Matthew 26–56); they were hiding behind closed doors on the day of His resurrection (John 20:19). According to scripture, they feared that the Jewish leaders who succeeded in having Jesus killed would also come after them.

Author's Perspective

What if I had been there when the religious leaders who wanted Christ dead went after Him, arrested Him, submitted Him to a sham trial, mocked and spit on Him, and screamed for His crucifixion? To be honest, I might have distanced myself and sought safety in the throng of enemies of everything He stood for. I'd have to think about it.

I admire the incredible bravery of John, who went all the way to the high-danger zone of the cross with Jesus, and I cringe to think of my dominant and persistent longing for safety. God, I really need your forgiveness; I cannot be like that.

CHAPTER 3

JESUS RACES TO FIND HIS RENEGADE DISCIPLES

On that long-ago morning after Passover Sabbath when Jesus arose from the grave and people were searching for His body, controversy hinged on two starkly different possibilities: If the body of the massacred Jesus Christ were to be found, stories of His resurrection would die as summer grass withers in the heat, based on the assumption that no rational person would believe in a dead Savior.

The disciples themselves, if they had been left in the dark about what happened to Jesus after His Crucifixion, would not have ended their vocations and embarked on lifelong missions to spread the Gospel. To think they did so, without financial compensation, other than sporadic private donations. All of them except John ran into hiding behind locked doors at the time Jesus was arrested, when they realized Jewish leaders were getting ready to hang Him on a cross on the rocky hill of Golgotha (an Aramaic word for "skull").

The Galilean men who had answered Jesus's call to dedicate their lives to Him might have raced to find Him once the Crucifixion was over and His body removed from the cross. But the Gospels tell a different story. Jesus actually rushed to find them. His first act, after leaving the sepulcher, was to seek out His disciples, who were terrified of being arrested and killed by Roman soldiers. He instinctively knew where they were, and without as much as a knock, He walked through their barricaded door and greeted them, ***"Peace be with you."***

The men were shaken to their core. They stared at Him as if He were a ghost, and He quickly calmed them by inviting them to touch Him.

"Behold My hands and My feet, that it is Myself. Handle Me and see, for a spirit does not have flesh and bones as you see I have," He said. ***"Do you have anything here to eat?"*** They gave Him some broiled fish and honeycomb, which He ate in their company (Luke 24:38–43).

Jesus's sudden intrusion in their private place was a shock. Despite His recent predictions of how He would suffer, die, and return to life, they had not actually expected Him to go to the grave and come out of it alive. No one was known to have witnessed His resurrection, but the disciples became eyewitnesses to His resurrected life. His stature, His voice, His manner of speech, and even His request for food were altogether familiar to them.

They touched Him and were sure it was Him when they felt the scars of His beatings and Crucifixion. They talked with Him, ate with Him, and stayed around as He explained the Old Testament prophecies of the extreme suffering He would experience:

"These are the words which I spoke to you while I was still with you, that all things must be fulfilled which were written in the Law of Moses and the prophets and the Psalms concerning Me," He said to them. ***"Thus it is written, and thus it was necessary for the Christ to suffer and to rise from the dead on the third day, and that repentance and remission of sins should be preached in His name to all nations, beginning at Jerusalem. And you are***

witnesses of these things. Behold, I send the Promise of My Father upon you, but tarry in the city of Jerusalem until you are endued with power from on high" (Luke 24:44, 46–49).

The disciples, who had assumed Jesus had died just as their relatives and friends had died, never to be seen again on earth, emerged from shock to realize He had conquered death. How could they believe it? First-century Judaism had no concept of a single individual rising from the dead. In fact, Jesus is the only religious leader for whom extensive circumstances verify that he rose from the dead; all other religious leaders remained in their graves. And He was with them, talking about a coming event in which they would experience extraordinary power from on high.

Jesus Breathes the Holy Spirit into His Disciples

"Peace be with you," Jesus said again. ***"As the Father has sent me, I also send you."***

He knew the time had come for the disciples to be ordained for their global mission. He breathed the Holy Spirit into each of the men and said, ***"Receive ye the Holy Spirit. If you forgive anyone's sins, their sins are forgiven; if you do not forgive them, they are not forgiven"*** (John 20:21–22). The act of breathing the Holy Spirit into the disciples was reminiscent of that historic day when God formed Adam out of the dust of the earth and breathed into his nostrils the breath of life, and he became a living soul (Genesis 2:7). This event also may have been a step of preparation for Pentecost, when the hearts of believers would be filled with the Holy Spirit.

Ten of the twelve disciples were in the hideout when Jesus showed up. The absentees were Judas, who had committed suicide, and Thomas Didymus, a Galilean fisherman who had told the others he would not believe "unless I can see the nail prints in His hands, put my finger into the prints of the nails, and thrust my hand into the wounded side." Eight days later, Jesus gave Thomas that chance at another meeting with the disciples. Thomas reached out his hand, felt the scars, and was overcome by emotion as he recognized Christ.

"My Lord and my God," was Thomas's cry of confession. Once so obsessed with evidence, he was convinced once he saw Christ face to face and touched his scars. Thomas became a passionate missionary, who devoted his life to preaching the risen Christ in Parthia, Persia, and India.

In an earlier meeting with the disciples, Jesus granted them power to cast out unclean spirits and to heal all kinds of sickness. He commanded them, ***"Go to the lost sheep of the house of Israel [the Jews]. Heal the sick, cleanse the lepers, raise the dead, cast out demons. Freely you have received, freely give.***"

Amazingly, Jesus empowered the disciples to perform the same miracles that He Himself had performed. Anyone watching them in action could see the impact of the Holy Spirit in their ministries.

Those who were blessed by the Holy Spirit included Simon Peter and his brother Andrew, sons of Jonas from Capernaum in Galilee; James and his brother John, sons of Zebedee; Matthew, the tax collector from Capernaum; James, the son of Alphaeus; Barnabas from Cypress; Philip from Bethsaida near Capernaum; Bartholomew (Nathaniel), son of Tolmai from Cana of Galilee; Thaddaeus (or Jude Thaddaeus) from a Galilean village called Paneas; and Simon the Canaanite.

Jesus broadened his circle of disciples by commissioning seventy-two men to pave the way for His expanding ministry. They were assigned to travel two by two to preach the Kingdom of God and heal the sick in all the cities and towns where He Himself planned to go. Although the Bible does not list their names, church tradition suggests these three were among them: Mark the evangelist; Stephen, who would later become the first Christian martyr; and Barnabas, a missionary and church leader, whose positive and encouraging work for Christ is described in the books of Acts and 1 Corinthians.

In a warning that would send shivers down the backs of these men so close to the recent Crucifixion, Jesus said, ***"I am sending you out like lambs among wolves. Do not take a purse or bag or sandals, and do not greet anyone on the road. When you enter a house, first say 'Peace to this house.' If someone who promotes peace is there, your peace will rest on them; if not, it will return to you.... When you enter a town and are welcomed, eat what is offered to you. But whatever house you enter, first say, 'Peace to this house.' And if a son of peace is there, your peace will rest on it; if not, it will return to you. And remain in the same house, eating and drinking such things as they give, for the laborer is worthy of his wages. Do not go from house to house. Whatever city you enter, and they receive you, eat such things as are set before you. And heal the sick there, and say to them, 'The kingdom of God has come near to you.'***

"But whatever city you enter, and they do not receive you, go out into its streets and say, 'The very dust of your city which clings to us we wipe off against you. Nevertheless know this, that the kingdom of God has come near you. But I say to you that it will be more tolerable in that day for Sodom than for that city" (Luke 10:4–14).

As He prepared to send thc disciples into a hostile world, He knew they needed more than superficial faith to achieve world evangelism. They were smart, hardy men who knew how to make a living under harsh physical conditions and government oppression. But they needed extraordinary strength, inspiration, and a motive to leave all that was familiar to serve as full-time pastors, missionaries, and church builders in the face of adversaries who sought to destroy faith in Christ. Ambition would not be enough.

Jesus informed the disciples that He had important things to share with them before returning to His Father. He knew some of them had nagging doubts as to who He was. Their uncertainty may have been top of mind when he asked them to join Him on a mountaintop in Galilee and commanded them, ***"Stay in Jerusalem until you***

are endued with power from on high." They had received major clues to what He meant by power from on high.

"I tell you the truth," Jesus said. ***"It is to your advantage that I go away, for if I do not go away, the Helper* [also called Advocate] *will not come to you; but if I depart, I will send Him to you. And when He has come, He will convict the world of sin and of righteousness and of judgment; of sin, because they do not believe in Me; of righteousness because I go to My Father and you see Me no more; of judgment because the ruler of this world is judged. I have many things to say to you, but you cannot bear them now. However, when He, the Spirit of truth, has come, He will guide you into all truth"*** (John 16:7–13).

The night before His Crucifixion, He made a similar promise that when He was no longer living with them on earth, God the Holy Spirit would live within their hearts as an ever-present helper and guide. He told them the Holy Spirit would be sent to replace Himself on earth and thus fulfill His promise, ***"I will not leave you as orphans; I will come to you"*** (John 14:18).

Earlier in the same conversation with the disciples, Jesus said of Himself, ***"He that sent me is with me: the Father has not left me alone, for I do always those things that please Him."***

"If you love me, keep My commandments," He said. ***"And I will pray the Father, and He will give you another Helper, that He may abide with you forever—the Spirit of truth, whom the world cannot receive because it neither sees Him nor knows Him, but you know Him, for He dwells with you and will be in you."*** (Note the involvement of God the Father, God the Son [Jesus], and God the Holy Spirit in assuring that humankind will not be left alone.)

Jesus also informed the disciples that the Holy Spirit will not speak on His own authority but will speak only what He hears. ***"He will tell you things to come. He will glorify Me, for***

He will take of what is Mine and declare it to you." On a practical note, He also told the men the Holy Spirit ***"will bring to your remembrance whatsoever I have said to you."*** (Contemporary interpretation: Jesus will help us memorize His words in scripture and hide them in our hearts.)

In His final public prayer to His Father regarding the original disciples, Jesus said, ***"As You have sent me into the world, even so have I also sent them into the world"*** (John 17:18). The disciples became known as apostles once they were sent out.

Author's Perspective

The disciples had heard Jesus say He was preparing to return to His Father, and they could not bear to see Him leave. He reassured them, *"I will not leave you as orphans.... I will pray the Father, and He will give you another Helper, that He may abide with you forever—the Spirit of truth, whom the world cannot receive because it neither sees Him nor knows Him, but you know Him, for He dwells with you and will be in you."*

The pain of losing a spouse that you loved dearly is suffocating; it doesn't go away. I believe you can die of a broken heart, and I came terribly close. But I was rescued by the Holy Spirit, sent by God the Father to live in my heart as an ever-present comforter, advocate, and guide. I cannot fully explain how it works. I only know that He works.

No need to chase through the Holy Scripture and Bible commentaries to find out how to have the Holy Spirit live inside you. Believers have to do nothing more than ask Him to occupy you, and He does. The result is a happy heart, and I cannot put a price on it.

Modern Perspectives

Rick Warren, senior pastor of Saddleback Church, an evangelical megachurch in Lake Forest, California, and author of the best-selling book, *The Purpose Driven Life:*

"Only the Holy Spirit has the power to make the changes God wants to make in our lives.... We allow Christ to live through us ... through the choices we make. We choose to do the right thing in situations and then trust God's Spirit to give us His power, love, faith and wisdom to do it. Since God's Spirit lives inside of us, these things are always available for asking."

Billy Graham (1918–2018), international Christian evangelist:

The work of the Holy Spirit was brilliantly defined in the ministry of Billy Graham, who preached to millions in 185 nations and territories before his passing in 2018. In his book, *The Holy Spirit*, Graham said people have two great spiritual needs: for forgiveness and for goodness. "To the great gift of forgiveness God adds the great gift of the Holy Spirit. He is the source of power who meets our need to escape from the miserable weakness that grips us. He gives us the power to be truly good."

Watchman Nee (Ni Tuosheng) (1903–1972) Chinese Christian pastor:

Persecuted and imprisoned for his ministry in China, Watchman Nee reached millions through his sermons and books describing the powerful inner presence of the Spirit of God. In an effort to describe the universal impact of the risen Christ, he wrote, "Our old history ends with the cross; our new history begins with the resurrection." Nee spent the last twenty years of his life in a Chinese prison.

CHAPTER 4

JESUS SHOULDERS THE COLLECTIVE WEIGHT OF HUMAN SIN

Not long after the temple-cleansing episode and after an illegal night-time trial before the Sanhedrin and torturous beatings that left Jesus bloodied and bruised, He was nailed to the cross amid hundreds of rough wooden crosses stretched across the Hill of Golgotha. A Roman soldier thrust a spear into His side, causing blood and water to flow out. Drops of blood trickled down from the crown of thorns pressed into His head and from the spikes in His wrists and feet.

A centurion, distinguished by the thick plume on his shining helmet, was stationed at the cross at the time Jesus prayed, ***"Father, forgive them, for they know not what they do."*** The centurion also heard Him cry out with a loud voice, ***"It is finished. Father, into your hands I commend my spirit."*** He was there when Jesus bowed his head and died (Luke 23:46–47).

Jesus's body would probably have been left on the cross, open to the elements and wild animals, or thrown to the dogs, if not for Joseph, a man from the Judean town of Arimathea. Joseph audaciously went into the palace and asked Pilate for custody of the body. Once his request was granted, he arranged for Jesus to be brought to the rock tomb he had planned for himself.

Jesus knew exactly what was to happen to Him: how He would suffer and how He would die. After He cleansed the temple courtyard of corrupt money-changers and greedy salesmen, certain Jews asked Him, "What sign can you show us to prove your authority to do all this?" When He responded, ***"Destroy this temple, and I will raise it again in three days,"*** they retorted, "It has taken forty-six years to build this temple, and you are going to raise it in three days?"

But the temple He had spoken of was His own body. Not until after He was raised from the dead did His disciples recall what He had predicted (John 2:18–22).

What brought Him to the point of being targeted for murder stemmed from Judaism's rock-hard resistance to any non-Jewish religion. Thus Jesus, Who said He was the Son of God sent to carry out His Father's will on earth (Luke 2:41–52), ran up against fiercely proud champions of the ancient faith.

Jewish leaders could see nothing about Him that warranted their esteem, much less their worship. To the Israeli Jews, He was the son of a carpenter raised in a peasant village by a Jewish couple seen frequently in the synagogue and at the temple. But He was not necessarily a peasant. He grew up in Nazareth at a time when it was closely connected to the sophisticated Greco-Roman city of Sepphoris, known as the jewel of the Galilee and as a popular site of silk trade. Sepphoris was only four miles from Nazareth, and it is likely that Jesus rubbed shoulders there with wealthy pro-Roman Jews, Greeks, and people from as far west as Egypt and as far to the east as Persia and India. Ruins of the city can be seen on a hill in western Galilee.

In this tropical scenic area, Jesus preached often about the coming of the Kingdom of God, prompting many people to ask when they could expect this kingdom and where it would be located. The language of Mark 1:15 indicates God's reign is coming on earth. This scripture dovetails with the promise found repeatedly in the Hebrew prophecies, that God will come to reign on earth and will establish justice and peace for His people and for all nations.

People showed up in droves to hear His moving and imaginative parables on timeless life issues. Some of the stories are echoed today in literature and culture. For example, the prodigal son, who was forgiven and welcomed home by his loving father; the Jewish Samaritan, who saved the life of a man lying near death on the road by taking him to an inn and paying for his care; and the tiny mustard seed, used as a metaphor for faith that starts small and grows mightily until it can move mountains.

Many of His parables revealed God's end-of-time judgment of all people, including one tied to the fishing trade: ***"Again, the kingdom of heaven is like a dragnet that was cast into the sea and gathered some of every kind, which, when it was full, they drew to shore, and they sat down and gathered the good into vessels, but threw the bad away. So it will be at the end of the age. The angels will come forth, separate the wicked from among the just, and cast them into the furnace of fire. There will be wailing and gnashing of teeth"*** (Matthew 13:47–50).

Terrible Loss of John the Baptist, a Powerful Voice for God

Tragedy struck when John the Baptist was arrested and imprisoned after he condemned King Herod Antipater for his sinful and illegal marriage. Herod had married his brother's wife, Herodias, while he was married to the daughter of Aretas, the king of Nabatea, and he had zero tolerance for anyone who would speak or act against him.

Jesus began his ministry while John the Baptist was still in prison. He traveled from Galilee to Decapolis, Jerusalem, Judea, and beyond the Jordan River, teaching in the synagogues and healing people of diseases and torments. Matthew's Gospel reports He attracted multitudes as He healed people who were demon-possessed or suffered with epilepsy or paralysis. He was still trailed by a multitude as He led His disciples to a grassy hilltop rising out of the Sea of Galilee and preached the message later called the Sermon on the Mount.

In that famous sermon, which Saint Augustine described as "a perfect standard of the Christian life," He declared His purpose to fulfill the Old Testament law, not to abolish it, and to uphold God's laws, including the Ten Commandments, the Lord's key moral and ethical principles. He emphasized the merciful forgiveness and grace of God for every believer seeking everlasting life in heaven (Matthew 5–7). He spoke of comfort, through the Holy Spirit, to people who are grieving or struggling to survive poverty or enduring persecution, including the oppressive government that controlled their daily lives.

Jesus also informed the people of choices everyone must make: to serve God or to serve mammon (the world), since it is impossible to do both, and to follow the narrow road (the Gospel way) that leads to life instead of the heavily traveled, popular road that leads to destruction.

He challenged not only the people on the hillside that day but a much larger audience: ***"Whoever hears these sayings of Mine and does them, I will liken him to a wise man, who built his house on the rock, and the rains descended, the floods came, and the winds blew and beat on that house, and it did not fall, for it was founded on the rock [referring to Himself]. "But everyone who hears these sayings of Mine and does not do them, will be like a foolish man who built his house on the sand"*** (Matthew 7:24–27).

Augustine's critique of the sermon bears significant weight; as an early Christian theologian and philosopher, he was one of the most important figures in the development of Western civilization. In the year 393, he wrote a commentary in which he said the eight Beatitudes (expressions of God-given happiness) at the opening of this sermon are pronouncements of the perfect moral law that was hidden in the Old Testament and unveiled by Christ in the New Testament.

Augustine answered a frequently asked question of why Jesus would declare, ***"Blessed are the poor in spirit, for theirs is the kingdom of heaven."*** In his quaint Old English, he explained, "Who does not know that the proud are spoken of as puffed up, as if swelled out with wind? And hence also that expression of the apostle, 'Knowledge puffeth up, but charity edifieth.' And 'the poor in spirit' are rightly understood here, as meaning the humble and God-fearing, i.e. those who have not the spirit which puffeth up. Nor ought blessedness to begin at any other point whatever, if indeed it is to attain unto the highest wisdom; but the fear of the Lord is the beginning of wisdom; for, on the other hand also, 'pride' is entitled the beginning of all sin. Let the proud, therefore, seek after and love the kingdoms of the earth, but 'blessed are the poor in spirit, for theirs is the kingdom of heaven."

Jesus presented two distinguishing life goals for all believers: ***"You are the salt of the earth"*** and ***"You are the light of the world; a city that is set on a hill cannot be hidden"*** (Matthew 5:13–14). Jesus said a disciple who does not live out the values of the kingdom is like unsalty salt, virtually useless and fit to be thrown out and trodden under foot. He cast unsalty salt in the same category as the scraggly fig tree that He cursed because it bore no fruit. In contrast, pure salt, which does not spoil or degenerate, is known for its preservative and wound-healing benefits. He used salt as an illustration for how believers are to safeguard the good aspects of society, comfort and heal the wounds of suffering people, and help to stop moral degeneration.

Unsavory Salt

The salt used in ancient times was not refined, and it often contained other chemicals in addition to sodium chloride. If the fraction useful for flavoring food was leached away by dampness, what remained was without value. It was sometimes strewn on paths like gravel, since it was "then good for nothing" (Matthew 5:13).

As Jesus presented Himself as ***"the light of the world,"*** He asked His followers to share the illuminating, soul-saving Gospel with others and give glory to God.

"You are the light of the world; a city that is set on a hill cannot be hidden, nor do they light a lamp and put it under a basket, but on a lampstand and it gives light to all who are in the house. Let your light shine so that they may see your good works and glorify your Father in heaven" (Matthew 5:14–16).

Crowds followed Him after the sermon as He resumed His healing mission. He healed a leper who called out to be cleansed, the paralyzed "dreadfully tormented" servant of a centurion in Capernaum, and Peter's mother-in-law, who was bedridden with fever. People came to Him with problems that seemed incurable: the man who had been blind from birth, ten lepers who called for help from a distance, the blind man who was tormented by demons, and a bedridden paralytic carried on a stretcher by his friends. All were healed.

Even natural disasters responded to His orders. During a fishing trip with the disciples on the Sea of Galilee, a sudden violent squall almost capsized their boat. The disciples clung to the mast, shaken off their feet, as wave after wave swept over them. The storm was shocking enough, although not uncommon on the low-lying Sea of Galilee surrounded by steep hills. Equally shocking to the disciples was the sight of Jesus sleeping on a pillow in the stern while the thrashing wind battered their craft. They shook Him awake.

"Teacher, do you not care that we are perishing?" they cried in desperation.

Jesus spoke to the sea, ***"Peace, be still."*** To His trembling companions, he asked, ***"Why are you so fearful? How is it that you have no faith?"***

Scene of Frequent Sudden Storms

The steep hills surrounding the small harp-shaped lake known as the Sea of Galilee can channel the winds and cause sudden dangerous storms upon the water's surface (Mark 4:37).

The wind died down; the churning water settled as the sun brightened. The men could scarcely believe what had happened. They marveled, "Who can this be, that even the winds and the sea obey Him?" (Matthew 8:27).

The disciples rowed to the other side of the lake, to the region of the Gadarenes opposite Galilee, where Jesus was met by demon-possessed men emerging from the tombs, men known to be so violent that people avoided the area. The men shouted, "What do you want with us? Have you come here to torture us before the appointed time? If you drive us out, send us into the herd of pigs" (referring to about two thousand pigs grazing nearby).

Jesus ordered the demons to enter the pigs, and when they did so, the entire herd ran down the steep bank and drowned in the lake. The men who had been tending the swine went into the town of Gadara and reported what had happened. Residents turned out en masse to meet Jesus and, apparently upset by the financial loss of their animals, begged Him to leave (Matthew 8:32–34).

Author's Perspective

As a Christian, I'm expected to be "the salt of the earth" and "the light of the world." I realize that when Jesus issued this appeal in His Sermon on the Mount, He meant it for believers everywhere at all times. I can't shrug it off simply because I consider it impossibly idealistic. Could I ever demonstrate these characteristics in my life in a world where people who talk about Jesus in public are generally ignored or assaulted? But popular acceptance is not a worthy goal for a Christian; it's about finding ways to help people know Him.

Finally, it dawned on me that as salt and light are indispensable to life, Christians are expected to make an indispensable impact on our culture: to be what the world needs most: peacemakers, loving, compassionate, honest, diligent, and helpful. The power to impact others is not so much in what we do but in who we are. We can see the suffering and the needs in people around us, and we can help many of them.

Obviously, if sin contaminates my life, others will see no need for Christ because what difference does it make? On the flip side, if what I say and do, and the attitudes I express, reflect the beauty and compassionate goodness of Christ, I can point some people to Him. I can be one small part of revealing the truth that is often hidden by darkness. It can be hard, but I'm called to action.

CHAPTER 5

JOHN THE BAPTIST ENDS THE ERA OF OLD TESTAMENT PROPHETS

John the Baptist was kept under lock and key in a dungeon in Jordan for two years before he met the ultimate punishment for having criticized King Herod's unlawful marriage. At the king's grand birthday banquet, his stepdaughter, Salome, entertained the crowd with an exotic solo dance. Herod was so entranced that he swore an oath to give the girl anything she wanted, up to half his kingdom.

The lovely dancer told her mother, Herodias, about the offer, and she took advantage of the chance to take horrible revenge; she asked for John's head on a charger (Mark 6:24–25).

King Herod made good on his oath and sent an executioner to the prison to behead the prophet, who had bravely spoken truth to power. John was in the prime of his life and the last in a long line of Old Testament prophets when his voice was stilled. John's disciples came and took his body and buried it. In the annals of Christian history, he is described as a highly effective prophet, who taught that the judgment of God was "at hand." He was a humble forerunner for Jesus Christ. He spoke often of Him as the One coming, Who will baptize believers with the Holy Spirit.

Jesus was grief-stricken over the death of his cousin and close friend, who knew Him so well and understood His mission. He boarded a ship and sailed to the far shore of the Sea of Galilee, expecting to be alone. But a great multitude of people trailed after Him on foot, and because of the many miracles they had seen Him perform, they clamored to get close to Him and have Him pray for their diseases. With prayer and patience, He healed all who came to Him.

As the sun began its descent in the desert, the disciples suggested that Jesus send the people into the nearest villages to buy food. But Jesus saw them as ***"sheep without a shepherd,"*** hungry after staying with him for three days with nothing to eat (Mark 6:30–34 and John 6).

He turned to Philip and asked, ***"Where shall we buy bread for these people to eat?"*** He said this to test him, for He already had a plan of action in mind.

Philip answered, "It would take more than half a year's wages to buy enough bread for each one to have a bite."

Another disciple, Andrew, said, "Here is a boy with five small barley loaves and two small fish, but how far will they go among so many?"

"Have the people sit down," Jesus said.

About five thousand men, plus women and children, sat down on the grassy slope. Jesus took the loaves, gave thanks to His Father, and with the help of the disciples, distributed bread to the people. He did the same with the fish, and when everyone had enough to eat, He asked His disciples to gather the leftovers so that none would be wasted. Matthew reports they took up twelve baskets full of the fragments.

The miracle is described in all four Gospels. Some of the people who were there were so impressed they called Jesus "the Prophet come into the world." He knew they intended to take Him by force and crown Him as their king, and He retreated to a mountain alone (John 6:14–15).

In a separate event reported only in the Gospels of Matthew and Mark, Jesus fed a crowd of four thousand men, along with women and children, with seven loaves of bread and a few fish. When the amazing meal ended, he got into a boat and went to the area of Magdala.

While miracles such as these convinced many Judean people that Jesus was the Messiah they had long waited for, Jewish authorities dismissed them as fakeries. The priests, elders, and scribes would tolerate no opposition to their powerful positions. They tightened their invisible noose to protect the interests of their sacred practices.

Jesus Presents Himself as an Answer to Prophecy and Meets Grave Threats

Jesus, like John the Baptist before Him, would go to His grave far too soon, in the minds of His followers, but in a public ministry of only three years, He did what the Holy Spirit had anointed Him to do and as the prophet Isaiah had predicted: ***"The Spirit of the Lord is upon Me, because He has anointed Me to preach good tidings to the poor; He has sent Me to heal the brokenhearted, to proclaim liberty to the captives and recovery of sight to the blind, to set at liberty those who are oppressed and to proclaim the acceptable year of the Lord"*** (referring to the Year of Jubilee, celebrated once every fifty years, when debts are forgiven, and slaves and servants are released (Isaiah 61 and Leviticus 25).

Ironically, when He stood before his hometown synagogue in Nazareth and read this prophecy and said He was the one anointed by God to preach, the congregants rose from their seats and chased him out. They intended to throw Him headfirst from a steep cliff at the edge of town, but He slipped away and left Nazareth for the fishing village of Capernaum at the northwest end of the Sea of Galilee. He continued, day after day, caring for the people as the Holy Spirit led Him to do.

Jesus knew His life was to end soon, and He took action to make sure His Gospel would not be forgotten. Just prior to His ascension, He called the disciples together in Galilee, where He gave them an assignment that would take the rest of their lives to carry out: ***"All authority has been given to Me in heaven and on earth. Go therefore and make disciples of all the nations, baptizing them in the name of the Father, of the Son and of the Holy Spirit"*** (Matthew 28:19–20).

The assignment, known as the Great Commission, was the last recorded personal instruction given by Jesus to His disciples. It is nothing less than His mega strategy for reaching the world with the Gospel through word of mouth and toilsome travels by camel, horse-drawn chariot, ship, and on foot, with donkeys as pack animals. His apostles would begin preaching the Word and performing the miracles God had empowered them to do. They would be progressively replaced over time, as is happening today, with vastly improved transportation systems, by a replenished corps of disciples sharing the love of Christ.

The brilliance of Christ's commission extends beyond His original disciples to call all believers, to the present day, to pass on the faith that was passed to them. As good trees bear good fruit, sincere Christians bear the fruit of their discipleship. He asked them to go, teach, baptize, forgive, and make disciples.

Jesus's first disciples, who had been despondent over His plan to return to heaven, felt immense relief when He told them He would not leave them as orphans but would come to them. Their readiness to work in faraway places was secured by their greater trust and His comforting words, ***"Let not your heart be troubled, neither let it be afraid."*** They had seen and heard too much to misunderstand

His motives. He appeared to have no personal ambition, as He spent His time caring for people who needed physical, mental, or spiritual help.

Jesus put up no fight for His life, but when the soldiers came to arrest Him and take him to the illegal night-time trial before the Sanhedrin, He told them that everything He had done, everything they accused Him of, was done in public. His entire earthly mission was transparent. ***"I spoke openly to the world. I always taught in synagogues and in the temple where the Jews always meet, and in secret I have said nothing."***

He also told Pilate at the trial, ***"My kingdom is not of this world. If my kingdom were of this world, then would my servants fight that I should not be delivered to the Jews, but now is my kingdom not from here"*** (John 18:36). He mentions the Kingdom of God fifty-three times in the Gospels. It is this message of a heavenly kingdom ruled by God that sounded subversive to the Jews and led them to nail Jesus to the cross.

When He proclaimed that the Kingdom of God was near, He was not talking about the coming of a place where God rules, but rather the dawning of God's kingly authority on earth. The reign of God, Jesus said, is at hand.

His resurrection was exhilarating to His followers and all who believed in Him. Even more gratifying was the fact He stayed around for forty days afterward to talk to people, including those He had known before. The only distressing aspect was His plan to return to His Father (John 16:16). The apostles, more than all others, suffered a heavy darkness of soul as they questioned how they could go on without Him on this earth. Their anxiety would be addressed in many ways near home and in lands foreign to those who first met Jesus and called Him Lord.

Jesus Creates a Sensational Fishing Event

John and Peter had amazing stories to tell of what they had seen with their own eyes and heard with their own ears, but not yet. They scarcely had time to think about public testimony before another surprising encounter with the risen Jesus at the Sea of Galilee. They were in a boat with five other apostles, heading for the shore at sunrise, after fishing all night with no results. In the morning haze, they noticed the silhouette of a man on the opposite shore.

"Children, have you any meat?" the man asked.

"No," they said, unaware of who He was.

"Cast your net on the right side of the ship and you'll find them," said the man.

John looked more intently at the man on the beach and shouted, "It is the Lord!"

Sun-bronzed arms were thrust into the cold water, and Peter scrambled onto the sand. There was Jesus grilling fish over a charcoal fire. The other disciples, about a hundred yards from the bank, pulled up in their boat as Peter strained to drag his seine net to the bank; it was filled with 153 large quivering fish. Jesus had turned their failed fishing trip into a bonanza. As they rowed closer to the shore, He invited them to join Him for breakfast, at which He would grill some of their fresh catch.

How could anyone outside their circle know they netted 153 fish? One probable answer is that John was so impressed by finding the fish where Jesus told them to cast their nets that he wrote a note about it, which would later become part of his Gospel (John 21:5–14). Or possibly, the men knew they would retell this fishing story in years to come and decided to take an exact count of the fish, lest it sound impossible to believe.

The miracle of the day was not the fish, but the resurrected Jesus showing up at the lake at the exact time the disciples decided to give up and go home. He was not a fisherman by trade, and He knew they were, but He had shown up for a reason. He jauntily suggested they cast their nets on the other side, and when they did so, they succeeded big time. They had enough left over to prepare salt-brine pickled sardines and garum, a fish sauce popular in the Roman Empire, to sell at the fish gate in Jerusalem.

Over-the-top success is often a mark of Christ's miracles, and there are remarkable parallels in the Old Testament. One example involved the miracle-working prophet, Elisha, in the Northern Kingdom of Israel. A distraught widow rushed to tell him, "Your servant, my husband, is dead. You know that your servant honored the Lord with fear. But the man to whom he owed money has come to take my two children to make them serve him."

Elisha asked how he could help and asked what she had in her house. She told him she had nothing of worth, except a jar of oil. He instructed her to go out and borrow as many empty jars as possible from her neighbors, then shut the door and fill the jars. Her sons brought the jars, and she began pouring oil from her original vessel, pouring and filling the jars one by one, until all were full. She informed Elisha of this miracle, and he told her, "Go and sell the oil and pay what you owe. You and your sons can live on the rest."

Fast-forward to the miraculous fishing trip at Galilee, and how Jesus changed the outcome. It was the third time Jesus spent time with the apostles after leaving the grave, and it turned out to be a historic day for Peter, who had cut back his fishing business in Capernaum to follow Him. While flames flickered from the red-hot coals, Jesus tested his resolve by singling him out and calling him by his Hebrew name, Simon:

"Simon, son of Jonah, do you love me?" (By referring to him as "son of Jonah," when Jonah was not his father, Jesus may have implied that he had the characteristics of the Hebrew prophet sent by God to warn residents of Nineveh of impending divine wrath.)

"Yes, Lord. You know that I love you."

"Tend my sheep," Jesus said before asking the same question a second time.

Peter repeated himself, "Yes, Lord. You know that I love you."

Again, Jesus asked Peter if he loved Him.

Peter could not stifle his grief, realizing he had actually denied Christ three times on the night of His betrayal, and now Jesus was asking the same question for the third time.

"Lord, You know all things; You know that I love You," Peter said.

"Feed my sheep."

As if to test the mettle of Peter's resolve, Jesus informed him of the extreme trials, including martyrdom, that he would face on the road ahead: ***"Most assuredly, I say to you, when you were younger, you girded yourself and walked where you wished, but when you are old, you will stretch out your hands and another will gird you and carry you where you do not wish."***

The once free-spirited Galilean fisherman was aware that Jesus knew his heart and how wrong-headed he had been in promising to follow Him anywhere but proving otherwise more than once. He had even denied knowing Jesus to some bystanders at the house of Caiaphas, the high priest, prior to the Lord's trial before the Sanhedrin. Jesus knew in advance that Peter would deny Him three times before the rooster crowed; He even told him so. On the night of his denials, he stayed at the priest's palace and was there when the rooster crowed just before dawn, prompting him to run into the courtyard to cry tears of shame.

Through three years of close friendship, Jesus knew another side of Peter that explained why He could forgive his foolish sins and trust him with the awesome task of caring for the poor and hungry so prevalent in the Roman Empire. Jesus remembered the time He was traveling with the disciples along the coast of Caesarea Philippi, and He asked them, ***"Who do men say that I, the Son of Man, am?"*** (His frequent reference to Himself as the Son of Man may refer to His humanity, as well as to Daniel's prophecy of a divine Son of Man, who will come at the end of the world to judge humankind and rule forever.)

The disciples responded, "Some say you are John the Baptist, some Elijah, others Jeremiah or one of the prophets."

But Peter blurted out, "You are the Christ, the Son of the living God" (Matthew 16:16).

Jesus exclaimed, ***"Simon, Son of Jonah, flesh and blood has not revealed it to you, but my Father in heaven. I say also to you that you are Peter [Petros] and on this rock [Petra], I will build my church and the gates of hell shall not prevail against it"*** (Matthew16:18).

In this situation, Jesus declared He will establish His church on the solid foundation of Peter's faith, revealed to him by God Himself.

As Peter examined his own soul, he may have wondered how God could tolerate him, much less call him to care for His people. Now, during this intimate fireside talk, Jesus actually let Peter know that He loved him, that He realized he had a good heart and could be trusted to take on one of the most challenging roles: sharing the Gospel with the world. By this time, he understood something about the cost of discipleship. He knew the hardships ahead would be more treacherous than storms capsizing his fishing boat. Yet he chose to answer His call to fish for the souls of men.

Meanwhile, the apostles were still in Jerusalem, waiting to find out what Jesus meant by His promise of ***"power from on high."*** Whatever this power is, it must be greater than the extraordinary gifts they had already received and greater than having the Holy

Spirit breathed into them, or else why would Jesus insist that they stay in the city?

The apostles were waiting when Jesus led them out as far as Bethany on the southeast slopes of Mount Olivet, within walking distance of Jerusalem. He blessed them, and they watched as He was carried up above the clouds beyond their sight. Standing next to them were two angels who asked, "You men of Galilee, why stand you gazing into heaven? This same Jesus, which is taken up from you into heaven, shall so come in like manner as you have seen Him go into heaven" (Acts 1:11).

Luke gives a vivid description of this historic moment, when Jesus left the earth by His own power in the presence of devoted apostles. Luke said the apostles worshipped Him, and He blessed them as He lifted off the ground. It would be the last time they would see Him in His resurrected body on earth. They returned to Jerusalem to continue praising God.

The apostles, along with Mary the mother of Jesus, His brothers, and more than a hundred other believers, went into an upper room to pray. The Bible says they prayed in unison, no doubt in a great sense of expectation for what they expected to encounter. Peter stood in their midst, spoke briefly of the death of Judas, and opened the procedure to replace him. The group nominated Barabbas (also called Justus) and Matthias, who had faithfully followed Christ from the time of His baptism to His resurrection and ascension. They prayed over these two respected believers and then cast lots. The decisive lot fell on Matthias of Bethlehem, who was then added to the eleven apostles. Several early converts to Christ—Matthias, Mary Magdalene, Mark, and Luke—also became devoted disciples.

These were the individuals who would spread Jesus's heart-transforming message across Judea, across the Roman Empire, and ultimately, across the world. Here is a list of the apostles and the locations of their missionary work:

Peter: Bulgaria; an area adjacent to the Black Sea near Turkey; Antioch; modern-day Georgia; and Rome. According to Christian tradition, he was crucified in Rome about AD 66.

James the Less, son of Alphaeus: Believed to have ministered in Syria. The Jewish historian Josephus reported that he was stoned and then clubbed to death in 63.

Andrew: Preached in the Soviet Union, Asia Minor, modern-day Turkey, and Greece. Reportedly crucified in 70.

Judas Thaddeus, also known as Jude: Revered by the Armenian Church as the Apostle to the Armenians. According to Eastern tradition, he converted the city of Edessa after healing its king. Martyred in Beirut, Lebanon, in 72.

Simon the Zealot: Often joined Judas Thaddeus in preaching as a team. Stories handed down from generation to generation indicate he ministered in Persia and was killed after refusing to sacrifice to the sun god. Martyred in 74.

Bartholomew (also known as Nathaniel): Widespread travels to India, back to Armenia, and to Ethiopia and southern Arabia. Martyred in 70.

Matthias: He was a disciple during Jesus's ministry. One tradition of the Greeks says he planted the faith about Cappadocia and on the coasts of the Caspian Sea. Stories handed down from generation to generation report he ministered in Syria with Andrew and was put to death by burning in 70.

Thomas: Said to have been active in the area east of Syria. Tradition has him traveling as far east as India, where the ancient Mar Thoma Christians revere him as their founder. They claim that he died there when pierced through with the spears of four soldiers. Tradition says he founded the first Christian church in India. Martyred in 70.

James the Greater, son of Zebedee and brother of John: Local missionary in Judea. According to Catholic tradition, he spread Christianity in the Iberian Peninsula. He was beheaded in Jerusalem in 44 or 45.

John: He and his brother, James (sons of Zebedee), were in Jesus's inner circle. At the cross, he responded to Jesus's request to take His mother, Mary, home with him and care for her as his own mother. He is said to have founded the churches of Smyrna, Pergamos, Sardis, Philadelphia, Laodicea, and Thyatira. From Ephesus, he was sent to Rome, where he was cast into a cauldron of boiling oil, from which he miraculously survived. Domitian banished him to the Isle of Patmos, where he wrote Revelation, the last book of the Bible. According to church tradition, he died in Ephesus at the age of ninety-three.

Matthew (Levi): Formerly a tax collector, he ministered in Persia and Ethiopia. He also wrote the first Gospel. Some reports say he was stabbed to death in Ethiopia, date uncertain.

Simon: The Bible calls him Simon the Zealot, perhaps a reference to his political affiliation. Later accounts depict him as a missionary to Persia, where he was martyred in 74.

Philip: Phrygia (Turkey) and Carthage in North Africa. In Asia Minor, he converted the wife of a Roman proconsul, and in retaliation, the proconsul had Philip cruelly put to death. Martyred in 54.

Paul of Tarsus, not one of the original disciples, was called by the risen Christ in a midday vision to deliver the Gospel to the Gentiles. The New Testament delineates at least fifty cities, most of them along the Mediterranean coast, during four major missionary journeys, from 33, when he was about thirty-one years old, to his martyrdom in Rome in 67 or 68.

Luke: A Gentile physician from Antioch who joined Paul's missions, he chronicled the development of the early church in the third Gospel and in the Acts of the Apostles.

Mark: Also called John, he was mentored by Peter, his likely source for writing the second Gospel. He traveled with Paul to Antioch. He founded the Church of Alexandria.

Mary Magdalene: Mary, from the town of Magdala, followed Jesus after He cured her of seven demons. She was first to see Him (near His tomb) after His resurrection and first to tell the disciples that He had risen from the dead.

CHAPTER 6

MIRACLES AND TRAGEDY ON STREETS OF JERUSALEM

Peter and the other apostles knew God the Holy Spirit because Jesus had literally breathed His presence into them in Jerusalem. The results were dramatic and lasting. This is the primary subject of Luke's book of Acts, sometimes called the book of the Holy Spirit, which describes five memorable instances of the Spirit's outpouring on believers.

The apostles performed many healings among the people and met often in Solomon's Colonnade, a long outside hallway framed by two rows of pillars, at the eastern end of the temple's outer court. No one else dared to join them, even though they were highly regarded by the people. More and more men and women publicly stated their belief in Jesus.

As word spread regarding the amazing cures, people brought the sick into the streets and laid them on beds and mats so that at least Peter's shadow might fall on some of them as he passed by. Crowds from neighboring towns brought their sick and those tormented by impure spirits, and all were healed (Acts 5:12–16). The apostles' achievements in the name of Jesus triggered jealousy among leading Sadducees, to the point they arrested and imprisoned them.

But during the night of the arrests, an angel of the Lord opened the prison doors and told the prisoners, "Go stand in the temple and speak to the people all the words of this life" (Acts 5:20).

The high priest and his associates called together the Sanhedrin and sent to the jail for the apostles. But they found no one there, despite the fact the jail was securely locked and guards were standing at the doors (Acts 5:23). The captain of the temple guard and the chief priests were at a loss. Someone told them that the men who had been jailed were in the temple courts, teaching the people. At that, the captain and his officers brought the apostles before the Sanhedrin to be questioned by the high priest, who reminded them that they were under orders not to teach in the name of Jesus.

Peter replied, "We must obey God rather than human beings."

The Jewish authorities were furious. They wanted to have the apostles put to death, but a respected Pharisee named Gamaliel, a doctor of Jewish law, gave them a stern word of caution.

"And now I say to you, keep away from these men and let them alone, for if this plan or this work is of men, it will come to nothing," he said. "But if it is of God, you cannot overthrow it—lest you even be found to fight against God" (Acts 5:38–39).

Persuaded by Gamaliel, the Sanhedrin had the apostles flogged, ordered them again not to speak in the name of Jesus, and set them free (Acts 5:40).

CHAPTER 7

PETER SPEAKS UNDER THE SPIRIT'S POWER; CHRISTIANITY IS BORN

On the day of Pentecost, fifty days after Christ's resurrection, with no apparent warning, a rushing, mighty wind swept through the upper room in Jerusalem where a hundred and twenty believers were united in prayer. The crowd included Jesus's mother, Mary, His brethren, eleven of His original disciples, and the seventy-two disciples He had dispatched as emissaries. They were waiting, as Jesus had asked them to do, for ***"power from on high."***

The prayer meeting included Galileans disrespected by the higher classes in Jerusalem, who would have been going about life as usual in the city. They had gathered here with a shared anticipation of the greater power that Jesus said they should wait for.

The thunderous wind was accompanied by an even stranger phenomenon: the people in the room saw divided tongues resembling fire, but not burning, on each of their heads, and all of them were filled with the Holy Spirit and began to speak in other languages, as the Spirit enabled them. The violent wind and tongues of fire were palpable symbols for the astounding effects of the invisible Holy Spirit. News spread to the streets, where thousands of local residents and visitors from distant Jewish communities were celebrating Passover, the historic occasion when Jewish people were freed from slavery in Egypt.

Pentecost was a major feast day; the steep narrow roads of the Holy City were congested with more than two hundred fifty thousand people, up from the usual population of about fifty thousand. Pilgrims had arrived from the eastern part of the Roman Empire, from as far west as Italy, and as far east as Babylonia, as well as from Mesopotamia and farther east from Parthia, Media, and Elam (present-day Iran). What better time for the outpouring of His Holy Spirit to reach people of many nationalities? Many of them heard conversations in their native languages and were astonished that the Galileans, who had never traveled outside Palestine, were speaking languages they had never studied.

"How is it," the visitors asked, "that we hear our own native languages being spoken?" Others loudly mocked them: "These men are full of new wine" (Acts 2:9 and 13).

Peter, previously known for his brash and unpredictable behavior, stood somberly in the midst of thc jostling throng with the apostles around him. Speaking in the common language, he sought to correct the sensational stories that were taking on a life of their own.

Pain and sadness were written on his pale face as he assured the crowd that no one was drunk at this time, the usual hour of morning prayer. To the contrary, he said, they were seeing the outcome of God's prophecy, eight hundred years prior, in the book of Joel: ***"You shall know that I am in the midst of Israel: I am the Lord your God and there is no other. My people shall never be put to shame. And it shall come to pass afterward that I will pour out my Spirit on all flesh; your sons and daughters shall prophesy, your old men shall dream dreams, your young men shall see visions, and also on My menservants***

and My maidservants I will pour out My Spirit in those days. And I will show wonder in the heavens and in the earth: blood and fire and pillars of smoke" (Joel 2:27–30).

Peter became the first person in history to publicly preach the resurrection of Jesus the Christ, and his speech had no soaring eloquence that might win him fame. Sorrow was reflected in his brooding dark eyes as he scanned the crowd of Passover celebrants and recognized many of the people who had screamed for Jesus to be crucified. His sermon sounded as if it had been written in his heart, through unspeakably painful memories of days with Jesus. His speech was an appeal to look with unshielded eyes at the horror they had seen here in the Holy City:

"Fellow Israelites, listen to this. Jesus of Nazareth was a man accredited by God to you by miracles and wonders and signs, which God did among you through Him, as you yourselves know. This man was handed over to you by God's deliberate plan and foreknowledge, and you, with the help of wicked men, put Him to death by nailing Him to the cross. But God raised Him from the dead because it was impossible for death to keep its hold on Him....

"Fellow Israelites, I can tell you confidently that the patriarch David died and was buried, and his tomb is here to this day. But he was a prophet and knew that God had promised him on oath that He would place one of his descendants on his throne. Seeing what was to come, he spoke of the resurrection of the Messiah, that He [Jesus] was not abandoned to the realm of the dead, nor did His body see decay.

"God has raised this Jesus to life, and we are all witnesses of it. Exalted to the right hand of God, He has received from the Father the promised Holy Spirit and has poured out what you now see and hear.... Therefore, let all Israel be assured of this: God has made this Jesus, whom you crucified, both Lord and Messiah" (Acts 2:22–33 NIV).

The people, who had listened in rapt attention, some of their faces tightly drawn in grief and guilt, began walking toward Peter and the other apostles. As if awakened from a long night's sleep and suddenly aware of truth they'd rather not know about, they came by the dozens, then in larger groups, convicted by the appalling fact of who had been killed.

"Brothers, what shall we do?" they asked the apostles.

Peter replied, "Repent and be baptized, every one of you, in the name of Jesus Christ for the forgiveness of your sins. And you_will receive the gift of the Holy Spirit. The promise is for you and for your children, and for all who are far off—for all whom the Lord our God will call" (Acts 2:38–39 NIV). The present and future tense of Peter's statement indicates no time limit on God's blessing of people with the power of the Holy Spirit. Nothing less could soothe their deeply wounded souls at this time and place. In the same way today, nothing is better able to heal the human heart.

The day of Pentecost, as Peter explained it, was the beginning of a continual outpouring of the Holy Spirit that would be available to all believers from that point on, Jews and Gentiles alike. As he and the other apostles would explain in years to come, the Holy Spirit enters the human heart and becomes a part of the believer. When He is in you, He cannot be separated from you. In God's scheme of things, a person blessed in this magnificent way possesses a guiding, comforting, strengthening inner presence that has no equal.

Peter pleaded with the people in Jerusalem to save themselves from "this corrupt generation." Before the day of Pentecost ended, some three thousand people declared their faith in Christ and were baptized: an explosive beginning. And this occurred at a time when there were only six thousand Pharisees in all of Judea. The baptismal pools on the Temple Mount, customarily used to baptize Gentile converts to Judaism, were put to use in baptizing Jewish converts to Jesus Christ.

Tears rained down cheeks as men and women who had confessed their sins underwent the cleansing ritual of baptism, symbolizing dying to one's self and being reborn in Christ. Thousands of new believers were inspired to help build the church.

The likeness of fire that descended that day was more powerful than the apostles may have imagined. The apostles and others who had prayed in unison for this great power had never seen or heard of such a phenomenon. They were "filled with awe at the many wonders and signs performed by the apostles" (Acts 2:43 NIV).

A greater impact would be observed over time, as the apostles experienced an ever-increasing measure of the Spirit's power in their hearts. They soon realized the infilling of the Spirit was not a temporary emotional high or jolt of excitement, but the beginning of a new life. The Teacher of all Teachers was inside them. The outcomes of the Holy Spirit's blessing on the apostles' lives and ministry were enduring and visible. They devoted themselves to teaching, praying, helping people in need, and winning souls to Christ.

Long before this birthday of Christianity in Jerusalem, the Holy Spirit regenerated and empowered people to serve God, but He did not permanently live inside the hearts of believers, as occurred at Pentecost. The first three thousand Christians organized themselves as the Nazarenes, named for the town of Nazareth where Jesus grew up, and they kept winning converts day after day.

Pentecost also has been said to signify a New Covenant relationship between us and God. The ascended Lord kept His promise that the apostles and other faithful believers would be filled with ***"power from on high."***

These Christ followers, moved by their common experience of the Holy Spirit, formed supportive communities of fellowship and sharing of meals, and they observed the Lord's Supper. They pooled their resources and sometimes sold their possessions to help those in need so that everyone was cared for: the sick, the widows, the lonely, and the socially outcast. They did not consider their movement a new religion but a renewal of Judaism.

The Bible does not tell the stories of all the 120 people whose hearts were occupied by God's Spirit on the incredible day of Pentecost. But scripture does reveal that Christ's closest followers possessed miraculous gifts of healing and devoted the rest of their lives to telling everyone they met about the resurrection of Christ. The Spirit led them, inspired them, motivated them with great vitality, strengthened and comforted them through unspeakable terrors, and sustained them to the end of their lives. The church, founded on the apostles' witness of Christ, became God's means of reaching the world with the Gospel.

Pentecost is historically proclaimed as the day when God sent His Holy Spirit to live permanently in the hearts of men and women who believe in the Gospel of Christ. But notwithstanding the phenomena of hard-driving wind, the likeness of fire on the heads of believers, and the sudden gift of language, no one can define the power of the Spirit inside the human heart. The Spirit's power is revealed in a person's life as it is lived.

The witness of the apostles yielded amazing fruit. Within fifty years, Christianity had spread across the Roman Empire and beyond. The growth has never stopped.

Scriptures Describe Outcomes of the Spirit's Invasion of the Human Heart

- The Holy Spirit is our Helper (also called the Comforter), like a sturdy lifeline constantly accessible in our hearts, who will be with us forever (John 1:46 and John 14:16).

- The Holy Spirit is our Advocate; He speaks to God for us and speaks to us (John 14:26).

- The Holy Spirit will guide us into all the truth, for He dwells with you and will be in you (John 16:13).

- The Holy Spirit will help us remember everything He has said to us (John 14:26).

- The Holy Spirit helps our infirmity (weaknesses), for we know not how to pray as we ought, but the Spirit Himself makes intercession for us with groanings that cannot be uttered (Romans 8:26).

- The Holy Spirit will convict unbelievers in regard to sin, righteousness, and judgment (John 16:8).

- The Spirit brings about our adoption as sons and daughters of God (Romans 8:14–15).

- The manifestation of the Spirit is given to each one for the profit of all: for to one is given the word of wisdom through the Spirit, to another the word of knowledge through the same Spirit, to another faith by the same Spirit, to another healing by the same Spirit, to another the working of miracles, to another prophecy, to another different kinds of tongues, to another the interpretation of tongues (1 Corinthians 7:10).

- The Holy Spirit is the sanctifier of souls (Philippians 1:6), the Helper, the Comforter, the Giver of Graces, who leads souls to the Father and the Son.

- The Holy Spirit seals the believer for salvation (Ephesians 1:13 and Ephesians 4:30).

CHAPTER 8

AMAZING HEALINGS IN THE NAME OF JESUS CHRIST

Peter and John were about to enter the temple for afternoon prayer when they met a middle-aged man who had been crippled for thirty-eight years (all his life) and was carried every day to the busy Beautiful gate, where he could beg for money. In his usual way, the man looked up at the men and asked if they would help him. Peter was ready for the moment.

"Silver or gold I do not have, but what I do have I give you. In the name of Jesus Christ of Nazareth, rise up and walk" (Acts 3:6).

Taking the man by the right hand, he helped him up, and instantly the man felt the tingling sensation of strength in his feet and ankles. He was so excited that he entered the temple courts, walking and jumping and praising God. Due to the fact he never walked before, never had a chance to develop muscle tone, he would have been dancing on thin legs. He probably danced in rags, since his lifelong disability had left him poor.

People at the scene recognized the man as the beggar they had seen sitting day after day at the temple gate; they were amazed at seeing him jump around. As he held onto Peter and John, most likely with a tight grip until he gained confidence in walking, the crowd of people ran toward them in the porch that is called Solomon's. There on Solomon's Colonnade, Peter was speaking again:

"Fellow Israelites, why does this surprise you? Why do you stare at us as if by our own power or godliness we made this man walk? The God of Abraham, Isaac, and Jacob, the God of our fathers, has glorified his servant Jesus. You handed Him over to be killed, and you disowned Him before Pilate, though he had decided to let Him go. You disowned the Holy and Righteous One and asked that a murderer be released to you. You killed the author of life, but God raised Him from the dead."

Turning attention back to the man who had just been healed, Peter declared, "By faith in the name of Jesus, this man whom you see and know was made strong. It is Jesus' name and the faith that comes through Him that has completely healed Him, as you can all see" (Acts 3:16 NIV).

Peter and John were fired up by the Holy Spirit burning inside them. Hour by hour, more people declared faith in Christ, until the number of believers swelled to about five thousand. But their ministry was temporarily stopped by the priests, the captain of the temple guard, and the Sadducees, who were greatly disturbed to hear the apostles proclaiming in Jesus the resurrection of the dead. The religious officers arrested Peter and John that evening and had them locked in the public jail overnight, planning to interrogate them the next day.

"By what power or what name did you do this?" the Jewish leaders asked the two men.

Peter responded, "Rulers and elders of the people, if we are being called to account today for an act of kindness shown to a man who was lame and are being asked how he was healed, then know this, you and all the people of Israel: It is by the name of Jesus Christ of Nazareth, whom you crucified but whom God raised from the dead, that this man stands before you healed. Jesus is the stone you builders rejected, which has become the cornerstone. Salvation is found in no one else, for there is no other name under heaven given to mankind by which we must be saved" (Acts 4:8 NIV).

When the Jewish authorities saw the courage of Peter and John, whom they considered uneducated, they were baffled. They realized these rather ordinary men had been with Jesus. With the former invalid standing and walking around, and with many people praising God for his healing, they had nothing critical to say.

The religious authorities ordered Peter and John not to speak or teach in the name of Jesus. The accused men responded, "We cannot help speaking about what we have seen and heard" (Acts 4:20). That day, the apostles were released with only stern warnings. They would not heed the warnings. They were Spirit-driven in a way too powerful for words, with a soul-winning agenda. As reported by Luke, many miraculous healings were performed by the apostles in the name of Jesus, in the face of relentless opposition.

Philip the disciple went to the city of Samaria to preach the good news of the Kingdom of God and of Christ, Who saves people from the penalties for their sins and heals their diseases. Many of the residents heeded his message, and people were healed of palsies, lameness, and unclean spirits. Luke reports there was great joy in that city (Acts 8:8 NIV).

But in that jubilant crowd, listening to every word, there was a sorcerer named Simon, who for many years had impressed the Samaritans with his magical performances. Many people actually considered him the great power of God. Simon trailed after Philip, watching him exercise a different kind of power that convinced people to believe in Jesus Christ and to be baptized. Then Simon himself became a believer and underwent baptism.

When the apostles in Jerusalem heard that the Samaritans had received the Word of God, they sent Peter and John to pray for all the converts to receive the Holy Spirit (Acts 8:14–15). The two apostles laid their hands on the new believers, and they received the Holy Spirit.

Sorcerer Offers to Pay for the Power of the Holy Spirit

When Simon saw that the Spirit was given when the apostles laid hands on people and prayed for them, he offered to pay Peter and John to grant him this same fantastic power. Like most sorcerers at the time, he made money through his magic. Perhaps he could make more if he had the power demonstrated through the hands of Peter. He wanted to know how much it cost.

Peter vented his anger at the sorcerer, saying, "May your money perish with you, because you thought you could buy the gift of God with money. You have no part or share in this ministry, because your heart is not right before God. Repent of this wickedness and pray to the Lord in the hope that He may forgive you for having such a thought in your heart. For I see that you are full of bitterness and captive to sin" (Acts 8:20–23 NIV).

Fearful, Simon begged Peter to pray to the Lord on his behalf so that Peter's words would not become reality. He had sinned grievously after being saved, and as Peter urged him, he knew he needed to repent (Acts 8:24).

Peter and John returned to Jerusalem, preaching the Gospel in many Samaritan villages. At the same time, an angel of the Lord instructed Philip to travel south from Jerusalem into the Gaza desert. On the way, Philip met a prominent Ethiopian eunuch, riding in a chariot headed for Jerusalem to worship; he was reading aloud scriptures from Isaiah the prophet. The Holy Spirit told him to speak to the eunuch. Walking briskly to keep pace with the chariot, he politely approached him and asked if he understood what he was reading.

"How can I, except some man should guide me?" asked the Ethiopian. He invited Philip to sit next to him in the chariot, and as they rode along, Philip shared all he knew about Jesus Christ, which happened to be the subject of Isaiah's prophecy (Isaiah 53). Through the conversation, the eunuch, who was a court official of the ruling Ethiopian monarch, came to believe that Jesus is the Son of God. Philip found a body of water and baptized him then and there.

For some reason, the Holy Spirit "caught away Philip," and the eunuch did not see him again (Acts 8:38–39). Philip went on toward Caesarea, preaching in cities along the way.

The apostles had a unique perspective from having lived and worked close to Jesus; they were simply telling others what they had seen and heard. Many Jewish people changed their religious viewpoint after hearing their eyewitness reports of healings by Jesus. Equally persuasive was the profound change in the apostles, from cowards hiding behind locked doors to fearless, articulate preachers of the risen Christ and the coming of God's kingdom on earth.

How could they go from a fearful state of self-protection to preaching the resurrection to people who were bent on killing those who based their faith on such a radical phenomenon? The answer is in the ***"power from on high"*** that entered the place where they prayed, occupied their hearts, and gave birth to uncommon courage.

> Take this as the secret of Christ's life in you. His Spirit dwells in your innermost spirit. Meditate on it, believe in it, and remember it until this glorious truth produces within you a holy fear and wonderment that the Holy Spirit indeed abides in you.
>
> —Watchman Nee (Ni Tuosheng), 1903–1972

CHAPTER 9

A HIGHLY EDUCATED ANTI-CHRISTIAN TERRORIST REPENTS

The apostles were deeply engaged in missionary service when the risen Christ intervened in the life of a prominent, well-educated Pharisee from Tarsus in Cilicia (now in Turkey), who was waging a murderous crusade against Jesus's followers. The man, known by both his Hebrew name (Saul) and his Greek name, Paulus (Paul), was the leader of a mutinous band of Jews traveling the countryside arresting and jailing believers with intent to kill them. He believed he was doing the will of God as he bound in chains or ropes people who had done nothing worse than declare their faith in Jesus, the Son of God.

Saul came to public attention in Jerusalem when the Jews, who aimed to wipe Christians off the map, arrested a young believer named Stephen, known for his compassionate care for widows. Stephen and six others had been selected to manage the daily food distribution to widows and families in need. He also preached that

Jesus of Nazareth, who had been executed and buried, had come back to life and claimed that he had seen Him face to face.

Saul, like most Jewish leaders, was enraged by Stephen's claims regarding Jesus. He was among the people who filled the benches at the synagogue to hear his eyewitness accounts. Saul and his friends realized they could not stand up against Stephen's wisdom or the Spirit by which he spoke about Jesus, and they bombarded him with false accusations. Temple guards arrested him on trumped-up charges of blasphemy against Moses and God; they arraigned him before the seventy-one judges serving on the Sanhedrin. When he defended the Gospel and described his insights into its meaning, his face reflected the inner presence of the Holy Spirit (Acts 6:15).

Jews spewing hatred for Stephen dragged him outside the city and rallied a mob to stone him. With ultimate grace, Stephen knelt and cried with a loud voice, "Lord, lay not this sin to their charge." The mobsters took off their cloaks and laid them at Saul's feet while they hurled the rocks that crushed Stephen and robbed him of his life. Saul looked on with approval, as Stephen was slain for his faith.

At the time Stephen was stoned in AD 34–35, a great persecution was raised against all who professed belief in Christ as the Messiah or as a prophet. About two thousand Christians were slain. English historian John Foxe (1517–1587), in his classic *Book of Martyrs*, describes a huge "army" of Jesus followers killed for refusing to deny their faith, from the murder of Stephen through the Reformation in England. He includes the original disciples, ten of whom were killed for claiming Jesus had risen from the dead.

Saul again had murder on his mind while traveling the wilderness road to Damascus, Syria, to arrest more Christians and bind them in chains. The date is estimated sometime between 33 and 36. He intended to bring his prisoners back to Jerusalem to be executed without a trial, but his brutal mind-set was shattered by an event that would change the trajectory of his life (Acts 9:1–18). On a clear, cloudless day, he was suddenly surrounded by a blazing light brighter than the midday sun. In the midst of that light, he met the resurrected Jesus Christ, who appeared to be close to his own age, and heard Him calling his name.

"Saul, Saul, why do you persecute me?"

"Who are you?" asked Saul, who would later be better known by his Greek name, Paul. His traveling companions heard the voice but did not see who was speaking.

"I am Jesus, whom you are persecuting. It is hard for you to kick against the goads." (In modern street talk, you are shooting yourself in the foot and it hurts.)

"Lord, what will you have me to do?"

"Arise and go into the city and it shall be told you what you must do" (Acts 9:6).

Paul did not question the order. Before this day, he believed he was helping God by crushing the upstart religion that threatened the ancient faith he revered. He had watched in disgust as Jesus's followers were praised for healing the sick and the lame, and had viewed them with contempt as they preached against immorality. Now, after meeting the risen Christ, he looked at everything with eyes opened to the truth. He had talked to Him and heard His call to a huge assignment. He was stunned by the fact that Jesus knew his name, knew what he was doing, and was changing his heart and mind at a dizzying pace.

One moment, and everything was different. Paul was destined to be a missionary for Christ.

He could not see where he was going and had to be led into Damascus, where he stayed three days without food or drink. A disciple of Christ named Ananias had been instructed by God in a vision to go to the street called Straight, a Roman road called Via Recta that bisected the city from east to west, and inquire at the house of Judas for a man called Saul of Tarsus (Paul), who is praying. Meanwhile, Paul experienced a vision of a man named Ananias coming in and putting his hand on him so that he might regain his sight (Acts 9:10–12).

Straight Street still exists today, running east to west in the old city of Damascus, with two partially preserved Roman gates.

At first, Ananias objected to Jesus's request, pointing out that Paul was directly responsible for killing Christians in Jerusalem. But Jesus directed him, ***"Go, for he is a chosen vessel of mine to bear my name before Gentiles, kings and the children of Israel. For I will show him how great things he must suffer for my name's sake."*** In time, Paul would know the thrill of being chosen as an ambassador for Christ, as well as the hardships of repeated suffering. God called him as a man of muscular, uncompromising faith to take the Gospel to obscure corners of the world, where the name of Jesus Christ had never been heard.

Just as Jesus ordered the events, Ananias laid hands on Paul and prayed that he would regain his sight and be blessed with the indwelling presence of the Holy Spirit. Immediately, scales fell from Paul's eyes, and he could see clearly again. He was baptized, apparently by Ananias, and stayed several days with the disciples in Damascus.

He began preaching that Christ was the resurrected Son of God and quickly became the target of attack by the Jews. He spoke courageously about Christ as the Messiah, sent by God to bring His Word of love, peace, and salvation to every human soul. He preached with fervent emotion, motivated by the Holy Spirit's burning presence within. He would later claim that he met the risen Christ with the same certainty as the original twelve disciples met Him, and that he was commissioned by Him in that Damascus Road encounter to be an evangelist to the Gentiles. Beyond that, Paul was blessed by the Holy Spirit as definitely as the 120 people at the upper-room prayer meeting on the day of Pentecost.

The calling of Christ on the Damascus Road, and the indwelling power of the Holy Spirit in his heart, would explain his many miraculous healings in Jesus's name. He persuaded thousands to believe in Jesus Christ as he preached across the Roman Empire. He traveled most of the time with companions, including Luke, Barnabas, Gaius, Aristarchus, and sometimes Timothy, and with the aid of pack animals to carry supplies. In four missionary journeys, he covered more than ten thousand miles and reached most of the Mediterranean world from Antioch, Syria, westward through modern-day Turkey and Greece, and back to Jerusalem. His homemade military-style tents were of significant benefit in his travel.

Paul expressed a clear mission statement in his letter to the Christians in Colossi: "Him we preach, warning every man and teaching every man in all wisdom, that we may present every man perfect in Christ Jesus. To this end I also labor, striving according to His working which works in me mightily" (Colossians 1:28–29).

His blinding-light encounter with Christ changed his worldview, to the point he no longer had a self-serving ambition; his new life's purpose was to help others know Christ. He dropped from high esteem among the governing Pharisees to the temporary status of highly despised turncoat against Judaism. Once he fully accepted the Gospel of Jesus, he lost the esteem of his father and his membership in the synagogue; he also lost his investment of time and study to earn his elite position. His personal losses and triumphs through Christ became the subjects of his powerful writings that form thirteen New Testament books, four of which were letters written from prison to the churches he helped to establish.

Paul described the eternal hope born in him through the risen Christ: "If there is no resurrection of the dead, the Christ is not risen. And if Christ is not risen, our preaching is in vain and your faith is vain" (1 Corinthians 13–14). "If in this life only we have hope in Christ, we are of all men the most pitiable. If the resurrection did not occur, mankind has been deceived."

In a more fatalistic tone, he wrote, "If, in the manner of men, I have fought with beasts at Ephesus, what advantage is it to me? If the dead do not rise, let us eat and drink, for tomorrow we die" (1 Corinthians 15:32).

Because of his previous overwhelming sin against Christ and his persecution of the church, Paul felt unworthy to be considered an apostle. He had come to realize that the greater his success in tormenting Christians, the worse his sin in opposing the will of God. In agony of soul, he referred to himself as the worst among sinners: "the least of all the Lord's people" (Ephesians 3:8).

But through the transforming grace of God, his indomitable will, and his unflagging commitment, he kept winning souls for Christ. He became a restless, unstoppable pioneer of Christianity's global expansion; in his senior years, he became known as the Apostle to the Nations and Apostle to the Gentiles. In the midst of soul-winning missions, he was repeatedly beaten by pagan enemies and Jews, who would not rest in their effort to crush every part and parcel of the Christian Gospel.

Paul was challenged to confront broad differences among opponents to the Gospel. While the Jewish religion was firmly fixed and predictable, the heathen systems of idol worship varied widely with the character of the gods that were worshipped, as well as with the prevailing philosophies and the intelligence or barbarism of the people. To reach them with new religious ideas, he had to first understand why they worshipped in the ways they did and determine what they found attractive in the mythological deities.

Threats against Paul grew heated in Damascus, where he spent several days with the disciples. He went into the synagogues, preaching the highly controversial good news that Christ, the Son of God, died for the eternal salvation of sinful people, and rose from the grave as the living Savior. Many of the people were confounded when they recognized the preacher was the same man who had been killing Christians. The governor under King Aretas had the entire city guarded so that it would be easy enough to arrest him. The violent mob, bent on killing Paul, might have succeeded if not for his disciples, who came to him in the dark of night and helped him escape, lowering him in a large sack-like fish basket over the city wall (Acts 9:25).

Ironically, Paul had arrived in Damascus with splendid regalia as the high priest's representative but now was leaving in the dead of night, in a fish basket. He was helped by the very people he had previously come to hurt.

Total Distrust among the Disciples in Jerusalem

Paul traveled to Jerusalem intending to join the apostles but was met with cold-shouldered resistance from these stalwart pioneers of the faith, who did not believe he was a believer and were actually afraid of him. A turnabout in their attitudes was achieved by a church leader and missionary named Joseph Barnabas, who brought Paul before the apostles to present strong support. Barnabas explained to them how Paul had met the risen Jesus Christ on the Damascus Road and had preached boldly in Damascus in His name.

But despite Paul's persuasive preaching of God's everlasting love and mercy for all people everywhere, he angered the Grecians, to the point they set out to kill him. This time, when the apostles learned of the plot, they helped Paul escape to Caesarea, Philippi, and from there to his native city of Tarsus.

Meanwhile, Peter was visiting believers in Lydda, a Roman city located along two major roads in the heart of Canaan, when he was introduced to a man named Aeneas, who had been bedridden with palsy for eight years. Peter prayed to Jesus for his healing, and at his instruction, Aeneas stood to his feet and made up his bed. When this wonderful event occurred, everyone who lived in Lydda and the beautiful fertile district of Saron declared their belief in Jesus.

Shortly afterward, in nearby Joppa, a port city on the Mediterranean Sea in Israel, Peter raised from the dead a disciple named Tabitha (also called Dorcas). Tabitha was well known for doing good deeds and helping the poor, and when her life was restored, many more people decided to believe in the Lord (Acts 9:41–42). In light of his former days as a Galilean fisherman and Christ's repeated calling for him to become a "fisher of men," it had to be thrilling to see so many souls saved. If he had stopped to think how many times he was beaten and his life was threatened, he would have to say the catch was hard-fought.

What followed next proved to be a turning point for the expansion of Christianity. A devout God-fearing Gentile in Caesarea named Cornelius, a centurion with the Italian regiment, had a vision in which an angel of God urged him to send men to Joppa to find Peter. At about the same time, Peter had a vision of heaven opening and something like a huge sheet being let down by its four corners, holding many kinds of four-footed animals, reptiles, and birds, some considered clean and others unclean. He heard a voice saying, ***"Rise, Peter; kill and eat."***

But Peter replied, "Not so, Lord, for I have never eaten anything that is common or unclean."

The voice spoke to him again: ***"What God has cleansed, you must not call common"*** (Acts 10:15).

The vision made no sense to Peter, until he heard that a Gentile named Cornelius, a man of generosity and compassion, well respected in the region, was seeking a chance to talk to him about Jesus Christ. His request was surprising at a time when the Gospel was preached only to the Jews. The Lord used the vision of clean and unclean food animals to impress upon Peter that whatever God says is pure is pure, and the analogy extends to the intrinsic value of people outside the Jewish faith.

"God has shown me that I should not call any man common or unclean," Peter said (Acts 10:28).

Peter accepted Cornelius's invitation to speak at his home, where a crowd of relatives and close friends were gathered. He explained to them all that he had seen and heard of Christ, how He was anointed by

God, went about helping people and healing all who were oppressed of the devil, how Jewish leaders called for His crucifixion, how God raised Him from the dead, and how Peter and the other apostles ate and drank with Him after He arose. He explained how Jesus came to redeem men and women from sin and to help them live as God's children.

While Peter spoke, the Holy Spirit fell upon all those who heard the message. The circumcised believers who had come with Peter were astonished that the gift of the Holy Spirit had been poured out, even on Gentiles. For they heard them speaking in tongues and praising God. Then Peter said, "Surely no one can stand in the way of their being baptized with water. They have received the Holy Spirit just as we have" (Acts 10:45–46 NIV).

Cornelius was saved that day, along with his family and friends. All of them were baptized in the name of the Lord. Six fellow Jewish believers who had accompanied Peter witnessed the Gentiles receiving the Holy Spirit.

News of the Gentiles' conversion did not sit well with circumcised Jews in Jerusalem, who confronted Peter with the awful fact that he had visited uncircumcised men and eaten with them. Peter told them about his vision, how he understood it to mean he should not call anyone common (e.g., Gentiles), and how the Holy Spirit fell on Cornelius and his household just as he was beginning to speak.

"So if God gave them the same gift [of the Spirit] He gave us who believed in the Lord Jesus Christ, who was I to think that I could stand in God's way?" Peter said (Acts 11:17 NIV).

When the critics heard this, they had no further objection. They praised God, saying, "So then, even to Gentiles God has granted repentance that leads to life" (Acts 11:18 NIV).

The Antioch church later helped settle a debate on the troubling question of whether Gentile converts to Christianity should be required to obey Jewish law. The ultimate decision, by the Council at Jerusalem led by Paul and Barnabas, was that Gentile Christians faced no such requirement. The Gospel of Christ reached into Gentile lives where they lived. They did not have to deny their culture, learn a new language, eat certain foods and not others, attend Jewish feasts, or observe certain days and not others. Christianity is about a loving relationship with Jesus the Christ and living in the Spirit, not about extensive restrictions in everyday life.

Many Jews who Jerusalem after the murder of Stephen traveled to Phoenicia, as well as to the island nation of Cyprus and the metropolitan Greek city of Antioch, Syria, and preached to the Jews, prompting many to turn to the Lord. The good news of Jewish conversions reached the church in Jerusalem, which responded by sending Barnabas to encourage new believers and help to build up the church. Barnabas was better known for his gift of counseling than for his preaching and was often called the "Son of Encouragement" by the apostles.

Barnabas in turn recruited Paul, who had fled from Jerusalem to Tarsus. The two of them worked together for a year, teaching many people of Syria and strengthening the Gentile Christian church. In time, they would become well-known church planters.

The prosperous and wealthy city of Antioch, acclaimed for its grand civic monuments, architectural beauty, trade, and agriculture, would fill a historical niche as the place where Jesus's followers were first called Christians. It also was the starting point for three of Paul's missionary journeys (a fourth journey was to Malta and Rome). The city proved to be a huge challenge to the missionaries; they found it riddled with corruption and worship for Apollo, the youthful and athletic Olympian god of music, truth, prophecy, healing, the sun and light, poetry, and more. The famous pleasure grounds of Daphne (a minor goddess in Greek mythology) on the outskirts of the city included a brightly painted temple dedicated to Apollo.

King Herod Agrippa's Reign of Terror

About AD 44, Christians in the Roman Empire suffered tremendous shock when King Herod Agrippa I, who was then ruler of Judea and other parts of Palestine under the Romans, began a crusade of terror against the church. James, the brother of John, was one of the first casualties. He was beheaded with a sword. The Jews approved this atrocious crime, so the king arrested Peter and handed him over to four squads of four soldiers each, with plans to bring him out for a public trial after the Passover festival. (Agrippa I was the grandson of Herod the Great, who had tried to kill the infant Jesus.)

Once again, Peter was in prison under very frightening circumstances. But the king's plans were thwarted by Christians praying unceasingly for his release. As it turned out, the night before King Agrippa was to bring him to trial, an angel of God appeared in the cell where Peter was sleeping between two soldiers, bound with two chains and guarded by sentries at the entrance. A light shone in the cell, and the angel struck Peter on his side and woke him up.

"Quick, get up," the angel said, as the chains fell off Peter's wrists. "Put on your clothes and sandals. Wrap your cloak around you and follow me" (Acts 12:8 NIV).

Peter followed the angel out of the prison, thinking this could not be real; it must be a vision. They passed the first and second guards and came to the iron gate leading to the city. The gate opened by itself, and they walked through it. By the time they reached the end of the street, the angel disappeared.

Afterward, Peter said he realized without a doubt that the Lord sent his angel to rescue him from Herod's clutches. He went to the house of Mary, the mother of John (also called Mark), where many people were praying. He knocked at the outer entrance, and a servant named Rhoda answered the door. When she recognized Peter's voice, she was so ecstatic she ran back without opening it and called out, "Peter is at the door."

Some of the people told her she was out of her mind, but she kept insisting. Peter knocked again and again until someone opened the door and realized it really was him. He motioned for them to be quiet and then described how the Lord brought him out.

Peter asked the people to tell James and the other brothers and sisters about this, and he left for another place. Herod Agrippa ordered a thorough search for Peter, and when he failed to find him, he cross-examined the guards. He blamed the guards for allowing Peter to escape and ordered all of them to be executed.

Herod Agrippa met his own horrific fate soon afterward, after he gave a public address from his throne and called himself "the voice of a god, not of a man." Because Herod did not give praise to God, an angel struck him down; he was eaten by worms and died (Acts 12:20–23). The biblical account is confirmed by the secular historian, Josephus, who wrote that Herod suffered violent stomach pains for five days before he died at the age of fifty-four.

Against All Odds, Paul Wins Converts to Christ

The Word of God spread throughout the region of Pisidian Antioch, where Paul shared the Gospel of God sending His only Son, Jesus, to earth to teach the way of salvation. He and Barnabas spoke in the synagogues and drew huge crowds of people, who responded positively and asked for more, to the point that one Sabbath day, most of the city residents came to hear the Word of the Lord. Jewish leaders were so jealous that they stirred up persecution against the missionaries and expelled them from their region.

Paul and Barnabas shook the dust off their feet and went to the city of Iconium. They were filled with joy and with the Holy Spirit, and in this city, a great number of Jews and Greeks chose to believe in Christ. The wonderful outcome was short-lived, as Jews and some of the Gentiles sided against the apostles and plotted to assault and stone them. But fortunately, Paul and Barnabas heard about their plan and fled to the country surrounding the Lycaonian cities of Lystra and Derbe.

A most interesting event happened in Lystra, when Paul healed a man who had been crippled since his birth. Paul sensed that he had faith to be healed and said to him, "Stand up on your feet."

When the man jumped up and walked for the first time, witnesses shouted in the Lycaonian language, "The gods have come down to us in the likeness of men" (Acts 14:11). They called Barnabas Zeus (Jupiter), the mythological king of the Olympian gods who was said to control the weather, and they called Paul Hermes (Mercury), son of Zeus and messenger of the Olympian gods. The priest from the Zeus temple just outside the city brought bulls and wreaths to the city gates so that he and the crowd could offer sacrifices to these two incredible gods.

Paul and Barnabas ran into the crowd, tearing their clothes, and shouted, "Friends, why are you doing this? We are only human like you. We are bringing you good news, telling you to turn from these worthless things [i.e., idol worship] to the living God who made the heavens and the earth and the sea and everything in them. In the past, he let all nations go their own way. Yet he has not left himself without testimony. He has shown kindness by giving you rain from heaven and crops in their season; he provides you with plenty of food and fills your hearts with joy" (Acts 14:17 NIV).

Despite the good words, Paul was targeted for the most severe, painful punishment he had received to this time. Some of the Jews from Antioch and Iconium came and stirred the crowd against the apostles. They stoned Paul and dragged him outside the city, thinking he was dead.

Scripture indicates Paul appeared to be dead. But despite lacerating wounds from the rocks, he felt a surge of renewed strength, like a tidal wave. He did not have to wonder where God was in his hours of crisis. God's Spirit was in him.

He regained enough strength to travel with Barnabas to the city of Derbe, where they preached the Gospel and won a large number of disciples. They made return visits to Lystra, Iconium, and Antioch to encourage believers to remain true to the faith. They appointed elders in each church and committed them, with prayer and fasting, to the Lord. After preaching in several cities, they sailed back to Antioch, met with the congregation of Christians, and reported all that God had done through them and told how He had opened a door of faith to the Gentiles.

Christianity continued to grow in city after city, especially in Antioch, Syria, where Paul and Barnabas stayed a long time on their second visit. At one point, after an argument over whether to take Mark with them to visit the churches or not, they split into two different teams. Barnabas took Mark and sailed for Cyprus, while Paul chose Silas and went through Syria and Cilicia, strengthening the churches. All four of them continued to serve God with devotion and won new converts every day (Acts 16:1–5).

Paul was about forty-one years of age when he began his missionary journeys, following ten years of preaching and teaching in Tarsus. Once he began, he would visit some fifty cities in his missionary journeys, rising up time after time from vicious beatings, arrests, and prison terms; he repeatedly escaped death traps set by Jewish authorities. Despite the ardent devotion in his Spirit-filled heart, he could not have anticipated how rough the road would be when facing opponents who aimed to cripple or kill alleged offenders.

Luke, a physician and historian, recorded most of Paul's life of preaching, teaching, and healing, which rivals modern-day thrillers in the action adventure genre. That is, thrilling for readers who like to be kept on the edges of their seats, but it was no thrill for the protagonist in real life.

When Paul and Silas sailed from Neapolis to Philippi, a Roman colony in Macedonia, they were headed for a place of prayer when they met a female slave who made money for her owners by fortune-telling. She trailed after Paul and his companions, shouting over and over, "These men are servants of the Most High God, who are telling you the way to be saved." She kept repeating this for many days until Paul turned around and spoke directly to the demon that apparently possessed her. At his command, the spirit came out of her and left (Acts 16:18).

Owners of the fortune-teller turned violent once they realized their profitable slave was gone; with her gone, their power was diminished. They dragged Paul and Silas into the marketplace to face the authorities with a serious charge against them: "These men are Jews and are throwing our city into an uproar by advocating customs unlawful for us Romans to practice." The merchants reported that Paul and Silas were announcing a power greater than Caesar and were advocating a new and unapproved deity named Jesus, Who demanded loyalty among the people.

Paul and Silas Immobilized in Torturous Imprisonment

The missionaries would not get by with this threat to profit and power. A crowd of onlookers joined in the attack to silence Paul and Silas. The magistrates ordered them to be stripped naked and beaten unmercifully with rods that sliced into the skin; they threw them into an inner cell of the Philippian prison with their feet immobilized in wooden stocks fastened to the floor, so they had no room to move. The jailer was ordered to keep them under constant guard.

Unable to stand up, sit down, or lie down, their confinement aggravated the pain coursing through their battered and bloodied bodies. They were still restrained in the stocks at midnight when they experienced an urge, presumably from the Holy Spirit, Who had led them throughout their ministry, to pray and sing hymns to God. Despite the nerve-wracking agony of their beatings, their voices were unscathed. They were able to pray and sing.

What they said to each other is unknown, but they sang loudly, and the sound of their voices reached the jailer and the other prisoners.

Although their songs are not named in the Bible, they may have chosen one of the Psalms they sang in the synagogue. One that would fit well is Psalm 27: "The Lord is my light and my salvation, whom shall I fear? The Lord is the stronghold of my life—of whom shall I be afraid? When the wicked advance against me to devour me, it is my enemies and my foes who will stumble and fall. Though an army besiege me, my heart will not fear; though war break out against me, even then I will be confident" (the text of Psalm 27, sung in Hebrew, can be heard on YouTube).

CHAPTER 10

PAUL AND SILAS RESCUED WHEN GOD'S POWER ENTERS THE JAIL

What happened next is a narrowly averted tragedy described by Luke in the book of Acts. A violent earthquake shook the foundations of the Philippian prison, causing all the doors to fly open. The prisoners' chains and the stocks came loose. The guard woke up, and when he saw the prison doors open, he drew his sword and appeared ready to kill himself because he thought the prisoners had escaped, and he would be severely punished. But Paul shouted, "Don't harm yourself! We are all here."

The jailer rushed into the cell and fell to his knees trembling before Paul and Silas, who had not bothered to leave. He brought the two men, no longer chained, into the light and frantically asked, "Sirs, what must I do to be saved?"

"Believe in the Lord Jesus, and you will be saved," they replied, "you and your household." Paul and Silas shared the Word of God with the jailer, who then led them to a fountain where he washed their wounds, after which he and all his household declared their faith and were baptized (the jailer's family was obviously with him the entire time).

The jailer invited the two missionaries into his home and served them a meal. He was overjoyed that his family had heard the Gospel and decided Jesus Christ was indeed who Paul said he was. At daybreak, the magistrates sent officers to the jail with orders to release the men.

Paul surprised the officers by pointing out that they had been beaten publicly without a trial and thrown into prison, despite the fact their Roman citizenship exempted them from such punishment. Paul asked that instead of being released quietly, they should be escorted out. Their wish was granted, but instead of leaving the city as requested, they first visited Christians in the region to encourage them to keep their faith strong.

Later, in a letter written from another prison, Paul expressed his love for the Philippians: "I ask you, therefore, not to be discouraged because of my sufferings for you, which are your glory. For this reason, I kneel before the Father, from whom every family in heaven and on earth derives its name. I pray that out of His glorious riches He may strengthen you with power through His Spirit in your inner being so that Christ may dwell in your hearts through faith. And I pray that you, being rooted and established in love, may have power, together with all the Lord's holy people, to grasp how wide and long and high and deep is the love of Christ, and to know this love that surpasses knowledge—that you may be filled to the measure of all the fullness of God" (Ephesians 3:15–19 NIV).

Paul also shared with the Philippians his greatest source of strength: "I have learned the secret of being content in any and every situation, whether well fed or hungry, whether living in plenty or in want. I can do all things through Him who gives me strength" (Philippians 4:13 NIV).

Reflecting on the many challenges in his missionary journeys, he wrote, "Whatever were gains to me I now consider loss for the sake of Christ. What is more, I consider everything a loss because of the surpassing worth of knowing Christ Jesus my Lord, for whose sake I have lost all things. I consider them garbage, that I may gain Christ and be found in Him, not having a righteousness of my own that comes from the law, but that which is through faith in Christ—the righteousness that comes from God on the basis of faith ...

"I want to know Christ—yes, to know the power of His resurrection and participation in His sufferings, becoming like Him in His death, and so, somehow, attaining to the resurrection from the dead" (Philippians 3:7–10 NIV).

Paul describes Christ's resurrection as the way in which all believers in Him will one day be resurrected by God just as He was; those who trust in Christ will not be subjected in eternity to a half-human existence in just their souls but will experience the freedom of having a glorified soul and body.

In humility, Paul said he fell short of the holiness that God calls His children to attain but considered his life an ongoing journey aimed at reaching that high mark: "Not that I have already obtained all this, or have already arrived at my goal, but I press on to take hold of that for which Christ Jesus took hold of me. Brothers and sisters, I do not consider myself yet to have taken hold of it. But one thing I do: Forgetting what is behind and straining toward what is ahead, I press on toward the goal to win the prize for which God has called me heavenward in Christ Jesus" (Philippians 3:12–13 NIV).

He gave the Philippians one of his most comforting statements of what the mighty power and peace of God can plant within the human heart: "The Lord is near. Do not be anxious about anything, but in every situation, by prayer and petition, with thanksgiving, present your requests to God. And the peace of God, which transcends all understanding, will guard your hearts and your minds in Christ Jesus. Finally, brothers and sisters, whatever is true, whatever is lovely, whatever is admirable—if anything is excellent or praiseworthy, think about these things. Whatever you have learned or received or heard from me, or seen in me—put it into practice. And the God of peace will be with you" (Philippians 4:5–9 NIV).

CHAPTER 11

PAUL PRESENTS THE KNOWABLE GOD TO ELITE PHILOSOPHERS

Paul was not easily discouraged, but in 51, his spirit was provoked within him when he entered the fabled city of Athens, Greece, and found it given over to idolatry. Human-made idols of silver, bronze, and wood filled the marketplace, the temples, and the shrines. Paul knew they were not mere items of art; they were objects of worship.

The Spirit of the living God within Paul was a profound contrast to what he saw in the urban jungle of inert divine objects. He had come here from the town of Berea, Macedonia, where many people had been saved for Christ; he was waiting for his missionary partners, Silas and Timothy, to join him. He walked the streets like a tourist, taking note of the imposing buildings of fine stone masonry and architecture that revealed its former days of splendor. Even the Parthenon was adorned with larger-than-life statues of Athena, the goddess of wisdom, war, and crafts, also the daughter of Zeus. The city was named for her.

Along the streets, craftsmen were creating souvenir replicas of the gods, and vendors were selling them by the hundreds, fueling the popular obsession with idols: the sin for which God had punished the Israelites. Other locals were tending the opulent temples honoring gods and goddesses. Here and there were altars dedicated to themes such as Shame, Reason, and Virtue.

Paul was seeing for the first time the infrastructure of the city known as the university center of the world, former home of renowned philosophers Pericles, Demosthenes, Socrates, Plato, Aristotle, Sophocles, and Euripides. These were scholars whose patterns of thought about the human condition and life itself influenced education for centuries. Athens was long past its zenith and no longer a political seat, but it was still a center of art, beauty, culture, scholarly study, and debate. Professors and students came here from long distances to debate philosophical issues.

New worldviews and new gods frequently came into vogue in this academic city. Paul was overwrought with concern for the Athenians, who seemed gripped by the superstitions, fears, uncertainties, tensions, and turmoil that resulted from following false gods. He was stricken by the fact that human souls were being destroyed by pagan ideologies that led to emptiness and confusion.

Unwilling to stand idly by or simply go elsewhere, Paul felt driven by his conscience to talk to the people. He went into the synagogue and the marketplace and struck up conversations with Athenians about their religious beliefs and the ideals they found appealing in the gods they worshipped. He talked to them about Jesus, the Son of God sent into the world to save men and women from the penalties everyone deserves for sins against God, how He was crucified on a Roman cross at the urging of Jewish leaders and buried in a private rock tomb just outside Jerusalem, and how He arose from the grave three days later. Paul recounted in exciting detail how he had met the risen Jesus Christ and heard His voice in a vision on the Damascus Road.

His description of the resurrected Christ brought him into immediate conflict with the Athenians. Stoic and Epicurean philosophers peppered him with incisive questions, asking for more information about the "foreign divinities" he talked about.

The Stoics were pantheists who believed that everything is God; he does not exist as a separate entity but is in the rocks and trees. They prided themselves on their ability to accept whatever comes and handle it the best they could. Epicureans were atheists and materialists; they denied the existence of God or a life after death, and believed pleasure is the highest virtue, while pain is the opposite.

Prominent philosophers took hold of Paul and led him to Mars Hill to address the Areopagus, the high court of Athens. He was asked to explain his teachings, which were stirring controversy among people long accustomed to their religious rituals and the commercial industries linked to their gods and goddesses. Ahead of his lecture, he was mocked in the market square as a babbling fool and as a gutter sparrow, like a rogue who picks up scraps from the gutter or hawks other men's ideas because he is too lazy or dull to have his own.

On the highest point in Athens, before the world's leading philosophers, polytheists, and harsh critics, Paul confidently faced his audience. From where he stood, he could see the gleaming helmet, shield, and spear of the colossal statue of Athena. Although scarred and shrunken from repeated beatings, he held himself erect and resolute in the faith that had made him a new man. A Greek among Greeks, as highly educated in philosophy, ethics, and Greek culture as any in the crowd, and empowered by that constant inner presence, he drew instant attention with his personal greeting:

"People of Athens! I see that in every way you are very religious. For as I walked around and looked carefully at your objects of worship, I even found an altar with this inscription: **AGNOSTO THEOS** (To an Unknown God). So, you are ignorant of the very thing you worship ... and this is what I am going to proclaim to you. The God who made the world and everything in it is the Lord of heaven and earth, and does not live in temples built by human hands. And He is not served by human hands, as if He needed anything. Rather, He himself gives everyone life and breath and everything else" (Acts 17:22–25 NIV).

(The altar dedicated to an unknown god was found in 1820 on the Palatine Hill of Rome and is now exhibited in the Palatine Museum.)

"From one man He made all the nations, that they should inhabit the whole earth; and he marked out their appointed times in history and the boundaries of their lands," Paul continued (Acts 17:26–28 NIV). "God did this so that they would seek Him and perhaps reach out for Him and find Him, though He is not far from any one of us. For in Him we live and move and have our being. As some of your own poets have said, 'We are His offspring'" [quoting a line from *Phaenomena,* the ancient epic Greek poem by Aratus, to show the Athenians that their religion was tantamount to idolatry. The common English word *phenomenon* is derived from this Greek word for significant occurrence].

"Therefore, since we are God's offspring, we should not think that the divine being is like gold or silver or stone—an image made by human design and skill. In the past God overlooked such ignorance, but now He commands all people everywhere to repent. For He has set a day when He will judge the world with justice by the man He has appointed. He has given proof of this to everyone by raising Him from the dead" (Acts 17:29–31 NIV).

Paul spoke to the Athenian intellectuals in their own terms but exposed the weakness of their thinking in replacing God, the Creator of life, with handcrafted idols that symbolized nothing but barren concepts and in rejecting the greatest miracle of all time: the resurrection of God's Son, Jesus. He explained to them that God is not the projection of humanity; He is greater than men and women, and He created us. He is the maker and not the made. The real God is knowable.

As Luke described the event in Acts 17, the response to Paul's speech was disappointing. Some sneered at his talk about the resurrection, while others said they wanted to hear more on this subject. An unknown number of people became followers of Paul and believed in Jesus, and among them were two prominent people: Dionysius, a member of the Areopagus and a ruler of the city, and an aristocratic woman named Damaris.

There was no great movement for Christ in Athens, and Paul was not wanted in the city, which refused him license to preach. But a church was planted under excellent leadership and through these first believers, the powerful Spirit of God reached secluded areas of darkness where ignorance and evil were entrenched in the intellectual capital of the world.

Paul would not return here. He had no way of knowing that in a few hundred years, the Parthenon in Athens would become a Christian church and that Greece would become a sovereign state in which the national flag flying next to ruins of the Parthenon would be lowered to half-mast each Good Friday and raised on Easter Day in honor of Christ's resurrection. In Greece today, about 98 percent of the population is Christian Orthodox.

> "Put very simply, Satan's power in the world is everywhere. Yet wherever men and women walk in the Spirit, sensitive to the anointing they have from God, that power of his just evaporates. There is a line drawn by God, a boundary where by virtue of his own very presence, Satan's writ does not run. Let God occupy all the space Himself, and what room is left for the evil one?"
>
> Watchman Nee (Ni Tuosheng)

CHAPTER 12

CORINTH: A PLACE OF BREATHTAKING BEAUTY AND DEADLY SIN

Seven lofty fluted columns that once fronted the temple of Apollo, the god of light, stood out among the ruins of ancient Corinth when Paul entered the port city in AD 49 to begin eighteen months of missionary work. Strategic in planning his itinerary, he chose Corinth as a leading commercial center and as the largest (population about six hundred thousand) and most influential city-state in southern Greece. In all likelihood, his poetic soul was stirred by the remnants of fine classic Greek architecture, which had survived many earthquakes and the invasion of warriors, and by the magnificent reconstructions of the past century.

Paul had traveled only fifty miles west of Athens to reach this thriving new Roman colony, inhabited by permanent residents of many nationalities, plus large numbers of sailors, merchants, military veterans, men of adventure, slaves, and freedmen from all over the Roman Empire. There were enough Jews to justify a synagogue.

The absence of an established aristocracy tended to make the people democratic and intolerant of control.

Yet despite Corinth's impressive cosmopolitan status, the city was degraded by gross, uninhibited immorality and idolatry that were entwined with religious worship. The dark side of city life was on display at the temple of Aphrodite (Venus), goddess of love and beauty, and at three of her shrines served by thousands of prostitutes, as well as at numerous temples where animals were sacrificed to the idols. There were temples honoring other Greek gods, such as Poseidon (Neptune), lord and ruler of the sea; Demeter and Kore, goddesses of an ancient fertility cult; and Isis, the Egyptian goddess of magic and wisdom.

Even the popular Isthmian Games, ranked second to the Olympics and dedicated to Poseidon, were marred by bribery and other corruption at the time Paul preached in the city. Paul used the language of the competitive games to emphasize the need for self-control and discipline to win the eternal prize in the game of life.

"Do you not know that in a race all the runners run, but only one gets the prize? Run in such a way as to get the prize. Everyone who competes in the games goes into strict training. They do it to get a crown that will last forever. Therefore, I do not run like someone running aimlessly; I do not fight like a boxer beating the air. No, I strike a blow to my body and make it my slave so that after I have preached to others, I myself will not be disqualified for the prize" (1 Corinthians 9:24–27 NIV).

The religious marketplace bustled with artists designing and crafting models of the popular idols, and vendors hawked cuts of meat from sacrificed animals.

Visible even to a newcomer's eyes was the gulf between the upper classes, living in artistically decorated homes with luxurious furnishings, pools, gardens, arcades, and Roman baths surrounded by servants and slaves, and the lower tier of workers, struggling to survive in squalid dwellings that could easily collapse in a high wind.

Few people were middle class; if you were not rich, you were poor. Paul repeatedly reminded the church to care for those in poverty and to find ways to help the weak.

Thorny problems, due to widely diverse beliefs among the people, came to Paul's attention as he checked the pulse of the city. Sexual promiscuity had reached such large scale that Corinth had become a byword for sexual immorality. Corinthian girls were considered harlots, and to Corinthianize meant to live a promiscuous life. Paul faced a steep uphill battle to build a nucleus of believers who chose to follow the radically different lifestyle of a Christian.

In the first of his two letters to the Corinthians, Paul described the emotion he felt when he entered the city: "I came to you in weakness with great fear and trembling. My message and my preaching were not with wise and persuasive words, but with a demonstration of the [Holy] Spirit's power, so that your faith might not rest on human wisdom, but on God's power" (1 Corinthians 2:5 NIV).

Where could he make a dent in the sea of ignorance and resistance to the idea of a resurrected Jesus Christ, Son of God? His actions, described in 1 Corinthians, reveal he was as resourceful as he was tenacious. He began by preaching in the synagogue and in casual talk in the marketplace. There, and in his letters, he emphasized the mighty wisdom of God that reaches humans solely through His Holy Spirit:

"The person without the Spirit does not accept the things that come from the Spirit of God, but considers them foolishness, and cannot understand them because they are discerned only through the Spirit," he wrote. "The person with the Spirit makes judgments about all things, but such a person is not subject to merely human judgments, for who has known the mind of the Lord so as to instruct him? But we have the mind of Christ" (1 Corinthians 2:16 NIV). Paul's statement indicates that believers discern the spiritual messages of God.

Paul's letter of 1 Corinthians deals with his concerns that certain sins of the city, including idolatrous religion, were troubling the young church. The congregation had sent him letters describing serious divisions, quarreling, and jealousy in the church. They asked his guidance on how to deal with a case of incest, lawsuits among believers, sexual immorality, marital infidelity, questions about speaking in tongues, eating food sacrificed to idols, and behavioral freedoms versus restrictions. Paul addressed many of the issues from a big picture perspective, urging believers to recognize "we are co-workers in God's service; you are God's field, God's building."

Paul Links Building Construction Concepts to the Human Body

Using building construction as a metaphor for spiritual growth, he appealed to the Corinthians to drastically change the way they consider the human body, especially their own: "Each one should build with care. For no one can lay any foundation other than the one already laid, which is Jesus Christ. If anyone builds on this foundation using gold, silver, costly stones, wood, hay or straw, their work will be shown for what it is because the Day [of judgment] will bring it to light. It will be revealed with fire, and the fire will test the quality of each person's work" (1 Corinthians 3:10–13 NIV).

"Don't you know that you yourselves are God's temple and that God's Spirit dwells in your midst? If anyone destroys God's temple, God will destroy that person, for God's temple is sacred, and you together are that temple" (1 Corinthians 3:16–17 NIV).

In the same letter, Paul repeated, "Do you not know that your bodies are temples of the Holy Spirit, who is in you, whom you have received from God? You are not your own; you were bought at a price. Therefore, honor God with your bodies." He drew a clear verbal image of the Holy Spirit living inside a person instead of dwelling in buildings, even cathedrals or temples.

Paul used strong language to warn the Corinthian believers "not to associate with anyone who claims to be a brother or sister, but is sexually immoral or greedy, an idolater or slanderer, a drunkard or swindler. Do not even eat with such people" (1 Corinthians 5:11).

"Do not be deceived: Neither the sexually immoral nor idolaters nor adulterers nor men who have sex with men, nor thieves nor the greedy not drunkards nor slanderers nor swindlers will inherit the kingdom of God. And that is what some of you were. But you were washed, you were sanctified, you were justified in the name of the Lord Jesus Christ and by the Spirit of our God" (1 Corinthians 6:10–11 NIV). By using the word *sanctified*, Paul said the people were separated from the sins that had been prevalent in their lives, and they were living for God.

Paul realized how idolatry was deeply entrenched in the city, where Christians were greatly outnumbered by pagans, and he saw the damaging effects on families and community. How great the temptations must have been when idolatry was celebrated in pagan festivals and processions, heathen ceremonies in the theatres, and even at family dinner parties. He emphasized the power of God to help them see the pitfalls and resist: "No temptation has overtaken you except such as is common to mankind. And God is faithful; He will not let you to be tempted beyond what you can bear. But when you are tempted, He will also provide a way out so that you can endure it" (1 Corinthians 10:13 NIV).

Regarding personal freedoms, Paul highlighted the distinction to be made between actions that a believer is free to take versus the need to avoid decisions that might hurt another person. "Though I am free and belong to no one, I have made myself a slave to everyone to win as many as possible. To the Jews I became like a Jew [such as in manner of dress or in food choices] to win the Jews. To those under the law I became like one under the law, though I myself am not under the law, so as to win those under the law."

In 1 Corinthians 10:23 NIV, he wrote, "I have the right to do anything, you say—but not everything is beneficial. I have the right to do anything, but not everything is constructive [uplifting or strengthening]. No one should seek their own good, but the good of others."

"But beware lest somehow this liberty of yours become a stumbling block to those who are weak. For if anyone sees you who have knowledge eating in an idol's temple, will not the conscience of him who is weak be emboldened to eat those things offered to idols?" (1 Corinthians 8:9).

Critical limitations on Christian liberty became a major theme of Paul's teaching. His counsel to look out for the needs of others, even in daily activities, has timeless application to building communities of mutually-supportive people.

His work was boosted by his close friends, a Christian missionary couple named Priscilla and Aquila, who were among the Jews expelled from Rome in the year 49 by Emperor Claudius. When Paul found out they were professional tentmakers, the trade he had mastered as a teenager, he joined them in mass-producing heavy-duty tents of goat's hair fabric or linen and leather, manufactured in his native city of Tarsus. He sold enough tents to support much of his ministry. At the same timc, Priscilla and Aquila added their seasoned Christian faith to the missionary work and persuaded more people to believe in Christ.

Sneers and Surprise in Corinthian Synagogue

Paul stopped his tent-making after Silas and Timothy came from Macedonia to join him, bringing a financial gift from the Philippian Christians. In his exuberant way, he preached every Sabbath to Jews and Greeks in the synagogue, focusing on Jesus Christ, the Prince of Peace and Messiah sent to earth to save people from the sins that enslaved them. He spoke persuasively of how Jesus changes the hearts of sinners and shows them the way to please God and receive His promise of eternal life.

As in previous cities, his teaching of the resurrection of the crucified Christ was repeatedly scorned. Critics shouted at Paul and became so abusive that he shook out his clothes in protest and said to them, "Your blood be on your own heads! I am innocent. From now on, I will go to the Gentiles" (Acts 18:6).

He left the synagogue and went next door to the house of Titius Justus, a worshipper of God. Paul began to preach to people in Justus's spacious home, and the results were astounding. Crispus, the chief priest of the synagogue, and his entire household listened to the life stories of Jesus and decided to believe in Him. They were followed by many of the Corinthians, who declared their faith and were baptized (Acts 18:7–8).

Paul remained a target of angry Jews and could have become seriously discouraged, but for Christ's appearance to him in a vision. One night, the Lord said to him, ***"Do not be afraid; keep on speaking; do not be silent. For I am with you, and no one is going to attack and harm you, because I have many people in this city"*** (Acts 18:9–10 NIV).

God's assurance of protection helped Paul face a united attack by the Jews of Corinth, who brought him to a place of judgment before Junius Gallio, the proconsul of the Roman province of Achaia. As Paul was about to speak, Gallio said, "If you Jews were making a complaint about some misdemeanor or serious crime, it would be reasonable for me to listen to you. But since it involves questions about words and names and your own law, settle the matter yourselves. I will not be a judge of such matters." Gallio dismissed the charges.

Paul thought of Jesus saying to him in the night, ***"Do not be afraid,"*** and he knew who thwarted his enemies' vicious plans. He continued to preach boldly of the grace of God and to encourage believers to follow the way of love and seek the gifts of the Holy Spirit.

To questions about speaking in tongues, he emphasized the practical purpose of the gift to bring glory to God: "Anyone who speaks in a tongue does not speak to people, but to God. Indeed, no one understands them; they utter mysteries of the Spirit. Anyone who speaks in a tongue edifies [strengthens] themselves, but the one who prophesies edifies the church. I thank God that I speak in tongues more than all of you. But in the church, I would rather speak five intelligible words to instruct others than ten thousand words in a tongue" (1 Corinthians 14:18–19 NIV).

"There are different kinds of gifts, but the same [Holy] Spirit distributes them.... Now to each one the manifestations of the Spirit is given for the common good."

In a humorous vein, Paul said, "Unless you speak intelligible words with your tongue, how will anyone know what you are saying? You will just be speaking into the air."

Paul explained that the Holy Spirit determines the specific gifts that He will give to individuals: gifts of wisdom, knowledge, faith, healing, miraculous powers, prophecy, speaking in tongues, and interpretation of tongues (1 Corinthians 12). He also declared that without love, none of the gifts are worth anything.

The wickedness of Corinth had rippling effects on the people, and Paul longed for a unity of spirit and an uplifting, encouraging way of life. He presented to the Corinthians certain principles of God that he knew provide a better way. The message that sprang from his heart, now known as the Love chapter of the Bible (1 Corinthians 13), remains as dynamic today as when he wrote it. The passage is frequently read at weddings but has broader meaning than typically associated with love and marriage. It gives counsel for a life that matters in God's sight.

From the Pen of Paul

"If I speak in the tongues of men or of angels, but do not have love, I am only a resounding gong or a clanging cymbal.

If I have the gift of prophecy and can fathom all mysteries and all knowledge, and if I have a faith that can move mountains but do not have love, I am nothing.

If I give all I possess to the poor and give over my body to hardship that I may boast, but do not have love, I gain nothing.

Love is patient, love is kind. It does not envy, it does not boast, it is not proud.

It does not dishonor others, it is not self-seeking.

It is not easily angered, it keeps no record of wrongs.

Love does not delight in evil, but rejoices with the truth.

It always protects, always trusts, always hopes, always perseveres.

Love never fails. But where there are prophecies, they will cease;

where there are tongues, they will be stilled.

Where there is knowledge, it will pass away.

For we know in part and we prophesy in part, but when

completeness comes, what is in part disappears.

When I was a child, I talked like a child. When I became a man,

I put the ways of childhood behind me.

For now we see only a reflection as in a mirror; then we shall

see face to face.

Now I know in part; then I shall know fully, even as I am fully known.

And now these three remain: Faith, Hope and Love.

But the greatest of these is love."

Paul gave poetic expression to the preeminence of love, which echoes Jesus's concise response to a lawyer's question, "Which is the greatest commandment in the law?"

Jesus answered, ***"You shall love the Lord your God with all your heart, with all your soul and with all your mind. This is the first and great commandment. And the second is like it: You shall love your neighbor as yourself. On these two commandments hang all the Law and the Prophets"*** (Matthew 22:37–40).

Paul left Corinth in about 51. Despite the deep-seated paganism and debauchery of the city, it was here that he enjoyed one of his most successful ministries. He was succeeded by a devout Greek Christian evangelist named Apollos (not to be confused with the mythological god Apollo), who was well educated in the scripture and had a passionate desire to spread the Word of God. Apollos was a friend of Paul.

Today, remains of the ancient city lie about fifty miles west of Athens, at the eastern end of the Gulf of Corinth. Its final destruction occurred at the hands of the crusaders in the twelfth century.

CHAPTER 13

PAUL CHALLENGED TO SOLVE "WAR" BETWEEN LAW AND GRACE

Crisis arose in the early Christian churches of southern Galatia, when many Jewish converts were persuaded to weaken their Christian beliefs to accommodate Judaism's requirements to be circumcised and to obey the ritual and ceremonial laws of Moses.

The apostle Paul was stirred to anger when many of the people abandoned the values he had taught during visits in the large Roman province. Both Jewish and Greek church members had been baptized in the name of Jesus Christ and nurtured in the faith based on salvation by the grace of God, as opposed to salvation based on good works (Galatians 1:6–13).

Speaking often in the synagogues, Paul preached the Gospel he claimed to have received not from any man but by revelation from Jesus Christ. He openly shared with them the shameful time when he had worked intensely to destroy the church of God. Then he informed them of Christ's horrifying Crucifixion as a sacrifice for the sins of every person and the astonishing fact that after three days in the grave, He was raised from the dead by the Spirit of God. He told them how he met the risen Christ on the Damascus Road, talked with Him, and heard His personal calling to preach to the Gentiles.

The people listened attentively to Paul, and many decided to declare their faith in Jesus Christ and become part of the Christian movement.

Now, recalling several visits with the Christian congregations in Galatia, he was astonished to hear many had been persuaded by a different gospel, which he said was "no gospel at all." They had listened to a group of Judaizers, who taught that Jewish converts to Christianity were obligated to observe Jewish laws as well as the teachings of Christ. The men were expected to accept the religious rite of circumcision as a confirmation of their faith.

Paul began his response letter to the churches of Galatia with great emotion: "Grace and peace to you from God our Father and the Lord Jesus Christ, who gave Himself for our sins to rescue us from the present evil age, according to the will of our God and Father to whom be glory forever and ever....

"Evidently some people are throwing you into confusion and are trying to pervert the gospel of Christ. But even if we or an angel from heaven should preach a gospel other than the one we preached to you, let them be under God's curse" (Galatians 1:6–8 NIV).

Salvation is not earned by a person's work or good deeds, but by the grace of God, Paul explained. He asked the Galatians, "Does God give you His [Holy] Spirit and work miracles among you by the works of the law, or by your believing what you heard?.... Scripture foresaw that God would justify the Gentiles by faith and announced the Gospel in advance to Abraham: **'All nations will be blessed through you.'** So those who rely on faith are blessed along with Abraham, the man of faith" (Galatians 3:2–21 NIV).

Paul explained in his letter, "God sent His Son, born of a woman and born under the law, to redeem those who are under the law, that we might receive the adoption as sons. And because you are sons, God has sent the Spirit of His Son into our hearts, crying out, 'Abba, Father!' [an expression of humble admiration for God the Father]. Therefore, you are no longer a slave, but a son, and if a son, then an heir of God through Christ" (Galatians 4:4–7).

So why had the Israelites been given the Law of Moses in the first place, with its many ceremonies, rituals, and symbols?

"It is for freedom that Christ set us free; therefore, keep standing firm and do not be subject again to the yoke of slavery [dependence on obedience to the Law of Moses to govern daily life]. Behold I, Paul, say to you that if you receive circumcision, Christ will be of no benefit to you. And I testify again to every man who receives circumcision that he is under obligation to keep the whole law. You have been severed from Christ, you who are seeking to be justified by law; you have fallen from grace. For we through the Spirit, by faith, are waiting for the hope of righteousness. For in Christ Jesus neither circumcision nor uncircumcision means anything, but faith working through love.

"You, brethren, have been called to liberty; only do not use liberty as an opportunity for the flesh, but through love serve one another," he said. "For all the law is fulfilled in one word, even in this: **'You shall love your neighbor as yourself.'** But if you bite and devour one another, beware lest you be consumed by one another" (Galatians 5:14–15).

He appealed to the Galatians, "Walk in the Spirit, and you will not carry out the lust of the flesh [self-centered and self-driven life]. For the flesh lusts against the Spirit, and the Spirit against the flesh; for these are contrary to one another, so that you do not do the things that you wish. But if you are led by the Spirit, you are not under the law" (Galatians 5:16–18).

Many sins result from living to fulfill desires of the free, unrestricted self, Paul pointed out. He said deeds of the flesh are readily apparent: "immorality, impurity, sensuality, idolatry, sorcery, enmities, strife, jealousy, outbursts of anger, disputes, dissensions, factions, envying, drunkenness, carousing and things like these, of which I tell you beforehand, just as I also told you in times past, that those who practice such things will not inherit the kingdom of God."

In contrast, a person who lives and works by the Holy Spirit will show the results of that presence in his life. Paul emphasized at least nine characteristics that become obvious fruit in a person who lives by the Spirit: "love, joy, peace, patience, kindness, goodness, faithfulness, gentleness, self-control, against such there is no law" (Galatians 5:22–23).

"Those who are Christ's have crucified the flesh with its passions and desires," he continued. "If we live in the Spirit, let us walk in the Spirit" (Galatians 5:24–25).

Paul the apostle, who comes across in scripture as a sensitive soul who cares deeply for the people he nourishes in the love of Jesus, pulls out all stops in defense of the way of Christ, as he seeks to persuade the Galatians to turn their backs on false doctrine and lifeless gods.

"Do not be deceived; God is not mocked; for whatever a man sows, that he will also reap. For he who sows to his flesh will of the flesh reap corruption, but he who sows to the Spirit will of the Spirit reap everlasting life. And let us not grow weary while doing good, for in due season we shall reap if we do not lose heart" (Galatians 6:7–9).

In addition to Paul's teachings of life in the Spirit, the apostle John taught people how to avoid false teachers by "trying" the spirits to determine whether they are of God: "Every spirit that confesses that Jesus Christ is come in the flesh is of God; and every spirit that confesses not that Jesus Christ is come in the flesh is not of God: and this is that spirit of antichrist, whereof you have heard that it should come, and even now already is in the world. You are of God, little children, and have overcome them [false teachers] because greater is He that is in you than he that is in the world" (1 John 4:4).

In contemporary society, the Holy Spirit's impact on human life is described in this article by Glenn Newton, a Nazarene pastor at the Pleasant View Church of Christ in Pleasanton, California:

Does anyone know where all sin starts? It always starts in our minds; sin takes root in our mind and then the actions; the fruit of that sin comes in our actions. So God, knowing this, has given us the Holy Spirit to fill our hearts or our minds with His Spirit, so that we can kill this sin nature at its very root ... instead of being mindful of sin, now as we walk in step with the Holy Spirit, we are mindful of God, and what He wants for us and wants to do with us.

Paul ended his letter to the Galatians in a deeply emotional tone: "From now on let no one trouble me, for I bear in my body the marks of the Lord Jesus" (referring to deep, visible scars).

Anxious that his words be taken seriously, he pointed out, "See with what large letters I have written to you with my own hand!" This time, departing from his habitual use of a scribe, he wrote the letter himself with a reed pen on a sheet of papyrus.

CHAPTER 14

PAUL INTRODUCES THE POWERFUL HOLY SPIRIT TO PAGAN EPHESUS

The Greek city of Ephesus, on the coast of Ionia, boasted a remarkable combination of peaceful rolling hills studded by palms and pines, and one of the world's most majestic temples dedicated to Diana, the mythological goddess of the hunt, the moon, and childbirth. The temple took 220 years to build and was one of the seven great wonders of the world at the time of Paul's ministry. It marked Ephesus as the seat of the most magnificent form of idolatrous worship then practiced.

The city was rich, powerful, and influential, as were most of the cosmopolitan port cities where Paul concentrated his missionary work. The sumptuous temple of Diana, featuring 127 Ionic stone columns, was the glory of the city. Her statue in the temple, made of ivory and gold, and the handheld sculptures of her were crafted with multiple breasts, signifying she was the mother of all life. The cult of Diana was closely aligned with magic and with erotic rituals with prostitutes, who plied their trade on the streets at night. As goddess of light, she represented the moon, but she was also goddess of the dark kingdom of the dead; she was unforgiving and bloodthirsty.

The cult of Diana still had followers in England as late as the 1700s.

Once again, Christianity and an idolatry sustained by superstition and profit motive would conflict in a major way as Paul preached the Gospel of Christ in the synagogue, in the markets, and in the streets, wherever people came together. Dissension was unavoidable, for faith in Christ requires ending idol worship, abandoning immoral and unethical lifestyles, and closing commercial industries associated with the objects of false divinity.

At the core of the conflict was the difference between a society founded on God's distinctive moral standards of right and wrong, including the Ten Commandments and the Great Commandment, and a society informed by lifeless gods whose character and attributes, such as superhuman strength, control over nature, and forecasting the future, are shaped by the artists who design them. The imaginative Greeks wrote fanciful explanations of how the world began and created myths to explain just about every element of the human condition. They ranked the mythological gods according to their own imaginary hierarchy.

The values of Jesus Christ, the living Son of God, represented a huge culture change for people immersed in pagan worship since childhood. Before they could seriously consider faith in Him, they needed to realize that He offers much more to their lives than the erotic rituals, profits, social gains, and power involved in the worship of mythological gods. To worship Christ involves a new way of thinking and living with defined boundaries, not aimed at social status or power. His way is much more specific in its call to worship one God, the Creator of all things, and to live only for Him. So what was it about the mythological gods that attracted many of the ancient Ephesians?

Paul shared with the people a Gospel that reveals the glory of God, Who is holy above all and Who loves every person in every nation with an everlasting love, God, Who reveals who we are in His sight and how we can be forgiven of our sins and reconciled to Him. One God Who is concerned about all the issues and problems of life, in contrast to having a god for each issue.

Paul invited the Ephesians to walk in love as Christ loved us and to live like children of light, for the fruit of the Spirit is all goodness, righteousness, and truth. He warned them to avoid the darkness, where people pursue sinful lives unrestrained. He explained the critical differences between pagan ideologies, which often destroy individuals and families, and Christ's way, which inspires purpose-driven lives with a powerful anchor of strength in times of trouble, along with a blueprint for joyful, abundant life and an assurance of eternal life.

Conversions of people steeped in paganism reflected the unrivaled power of the Gospel to give people reasons to live for God. American historical writer Will Durant (1885–1981) said the Christian church prevailed over paganism because it offered a more attractive doctrine and because the church leaders addressed human needs better than their rivals.

A Mini Version of the Day of Pentecost in Ephesus

The Holy Spirit played a central role in strengthening the faith of twelve disciples of Jesus, whom Paul befriended after he entered Ephesus. As Luke describes the scene in Acts, Paul asked the Christians, "Did you receive the Holy Spirit when you believed?"

"No, we have not even heard that there is a Holy Spirit," they answered. They had heard nothing about the Spirit's outpour on believers on the day of Pentecost in Jerusalem.

"Then what baptism did you receive?" Paul asked.

"John's baptism," they said, referring to John the Baptist, who had baptized men and women in token of their repentance and their recognition that God's kingdom was imminent.

Paul explained the blessings that people enjoy when their hearts are filled with the love and power of the Holy Spirit. The dozen men, who had never been informed of God's Spirit, declared their belief in Jesus Christ and agreed to be baptized in His name. The baptismal ceremony may have taken place in the River Cayster, not far from the Temple of Artemis (Diana).

What followed has been described by Christian writer John Pollock as "like the day of Pentecost in Jerusalem over again. They spoke in tongues, praising and proclaiming the glories of the name of Jesus, then told everybody they met about the truths that suddenly had become clear to them in the Scriptures they already knew" (Pollock is author of *The Apostle: A Life of Paul*).

The Spirit-filled Christians, along with Aquila and Priscilla and their converts, formed the nucleus of a church when Paul went again to the synagogue to preach. For three months, he spoke boldly about the kingdom of God to Jews, some of whom were persuaded to believe. Others scoffed and slandered the way of Christ (Acts 19:8–9).

Among the fiercest opponents was Demetrius, a silversmith who made his living fabricating silver shrines of Diana. He stirred great anxiety among the craftsmen and workers of similar trades by pointing out how Paul was turning away their customers by declaring handmade gods were not gods at all. Demetrius warned the people that not only was their trade falling into disrepute, but it also appeared that the temple of the great goddess Diana, whom the world worshipped, would be despised and her magnificence destroyed (Acts 19:24–35).

Street rage grew into a loud, menacing mob in the city theatre and led to the arrest of Paul's travel companions. Paul wanted to go into the theatre and talk to the people but was held back by his protective friends. Ultimately, the tumult was calmed by a city clerk, who informed the crowd that Paul and his disciples had not robbed the temple and had not blasphemed the goddess Diana: "If Demetrius and his fellow craftsmen have a case against anyone, the courts are open and there are proconsuls. Let them bring charges against one another." With this and other words of counsel, he quieted and dismissed the crowd (Acts 19:37–41).

For the pagans, who depended on the business of idolatry for their livelihood or worshipped the idols they considered divine, the decision to follow Christ was a demanding, even sacrificial, prospect. Yet that choice was made by many of those who heard Paul talk about Christ, Who died for the sins of humankind and conquered death by returning to life. Paul, at this point, saw the beginning of a breakdown in the wall of hostility between Jews and Gentiles.

He preached, "I, the prisoner of the Lord, beseech you to walk worthy of the calling with which you are called, with all lowliness and gentleness, with longsuffering, bearing with one another in love endeavoring to keep the unity of the [Holy] Spirit in the bond of peace. There is one body and one Spirit, just as you were called in one hope of your calling; one Lord, one faith, one baptism, one God and Father of all, who is above all and through all, and in you all" (Ephesians 4:1–6).

He took the disciples with him and led daily discussions of the Gospel in the School of Tyrannus, located in a prestigious neighborhood. Paul held classes there during hours when the hall was empty. According to the book of Acts, "God did extraordinary miracles through Paul, so that even handkerchiefs and aprons that had touched him were taken to the sick, and their illnesses were cured and the evil spirits left them."

Some of the Jews were so impressed that they also tried to drive out evil spirits in the name of Jesus Christ, but they were quickly defeated. Several sons of a Jewish chief priest named Sceva tried doing this very thing. But one day, an evil spirit in a man told them, "Jesus I know, and Paul I know, but who are you?" At that, the man possessed by the evil spirit grabbed them all and beat them so severely that they ran out of the house, naked and bleeding. The incident prompted some of the people to hold the name of Jesus in higher esteem (Acts 19:11–17 NIV).

Most surprising was the group of sorcerers, who decided on their own to publicly burn their objects of worship and papyrus scrolls containing magical incantations and charms. They counted up the value of their books of magic, and it totaled fifty thousand drachmas (ancient Greek silver coins). They literally destroyed their own business, and through similar events, the word of the Lord grew mightily and prevailed (Acts 19:19–20).

Paul never lost sight of his sinful past; his sense of shame never diminished. Out of profound gratitude for God's mercy, and for considering him worthy to preach to the Gentiles, Paul reminded the Ephesians, "Through faith in Him, we may approach God with freedom and confidence." He expressed his heartfelt hopes for them in a prayer: "I pray that out of His glorious riches He may strengthen you with power through His [Holy] Spirit in your inner being, so that Christ may dwell in your hearts through faith. And I pray that you, being rooted and established in love, may have power, together with all the Lord's holy people, to grasp how wide and long and high and deep is the love of Christ—that you may be filled to the measure of all the fulness of God" (Ephesians 3:14–21 NIV).

Paul challenged the Ephesians to become spiritually mature and to make the world a better place. "We should no longer be children tossed to and fro and carried about with every wind of doctrine, by the trickery of men, in the craftiness of deceitful plotting."

Paul captured the essence of the life-changing Gospel, urging them to get rid of bitterness, rage, anger, brawling, and slander, along with every form of malice, to be "kind and compassionate to one another, forgiving each other, just as in Christ God forgave you. Follow God's example, therefore, as dearly loved children and walk in the way of love, just as Christ loved us and gave Himself up for us as a fragrant offering and sacrifice to God" (Ephesians 4:32–6:2 NIV).

He also taught, "Among you there must not be even a hint of sexual immorality, or of any kind of impurity, or of greed, because these are improper for God's holy people. Nor should there be obscenity, foolish talk or coarse joking, which are out of place, but rather, thanksgiving. For of this you can be sure—no immoral, impure or greedy person—such a person as an idolater—has any inheritance in the kingdom of Christ and of God" (Ephesians 5:4 NIV).

"Be very careful then how you live—not as unwise but as wise—making the most of every opportunity because the days are evil," he cautioned. His words indicated that, like Christ before him, he was keenly aware of the rapid march of time and tried to make the most of every day.

He emphasized the honorable, loving, and supportive relationships that should be maintained between husband and wife, parents and children, business owners and workers, slaves or servants and their masters. Regarding slaves, which were at that time commonly employed in many types of work, Paul did not publicly fight the long-established system, but knocked the props out from under it by calling for the loving treatment of servants. He delivered a twofold message in Ephesians 6:5–9 NIV:

"Slaves, obey your earthly masters with respect and fear, and with sincerity of heart, just as you would obey Christ. Obey them not only to win their favor when their eyes are on you, but as slaves of Christ, doing the will of God from your heart. Serve wholeheartedly as if you were serving the Lord, not people. because you know that the Lord will reward each one for whatever good they do, whether they are slave or free.

"And masters, treat your slaves in the same way. Do not threaten them, since you know who is both their Master and yours is in heaven, and there is no favoritism with Him."

Through the messages he preached in many settings, Paul declared the free man and the slave are of equal value in the eyes of God.

Consequently, the slave is not excluded from the hope of heaven or from being regarded as a child of God.

Military Armor Is Paul's Metaphor for Strength in Christian Life

While still in chains and confined under house arrest in Rome, Paul provided his fellow Christians in Ephesus with a motivational treatise on taking a strong, immovable stand for Christ while living in a world filled with "the forces of evil."

From the Pen of Paul

"Finally, be strong in the Lord and in His mighty power.

"Put on the whole armor of God, so that you can take your stand against the devil's schemes.

"For our struggle is not against flesh and blood, but against the rulers, against the authorities, against the powers of this dark world and against the spiritual forces of evil in the heavenly realms.

"Therefore, put on the full armor of God, so that when the day of evil comes, you may be able to stand your ground, and after you have done everything, to stand.

"Stand firm, then, with the belt of truth buckled around your waist, with the breastplate of righteousness in place, and with your feet fitted with the readiness that comes from the gospel of peace.

"In addition to all this, take up the shield of faith, with which you can extinguish all the flaming arrows of the evil one.

"Take the helmet of salvation and the sword of the Spirit, which is the word of God.

"And pray in the Spirit on all occasions with all kinds of prayers and requests. With all this in mind, be alert and always keep on praying for all the Lord's people.

"Pray also for me, that whenever I speak, words may be given me so that I will fearlessly make known the mystery of the gospel, for which I am an ambassador in chains. Pray that I may declare it fearlessly, as I should" (Ephesians 6:10–20 NIV).

Matthew Henry's *Commentary on the Whole Bible* notes that there is no protective armor for the back: nothing to defend those who turn back in Christian warfare. He further points out, "The Christian armor is made to be worn, and there is no putting off our armor till we have done our warfare, and finished our course."

The love that Paul inspired among the people of the church he founded in Ephesus was on open display the day he left the city. It turned out to be an emotional and bittersweet farewell, for the night before, a miracle happened at the hands of Paul, under the power of the Holy Spirit.

It was the first day of the week, and the disciples had come together with Paul to break bread. In the third-story meeting room, lighted by oil lamps, the group was engrossed in conversation. Paul was still preaching in the dim lamp light at around midnight when a young man named Eutychus fell asleep in the open windowsill. He lost his balance and fell onto the narrow street below. He was "taken up dead," but Paul ran down the steps, knelt and fell on him in an embrace, and said to those nearby, "Do not trouble yourselves, for his life is in him."

The people took the young man home alive and were greatly comforted (Acts 20:7–12).

Paul called for the elders of the Ephesian church and told them he was in a hurry to reach Jerusalem in time for the day of Pentecost. He said he planned to go there, not knowing what would happen to him, "except that the Holy Spirit testifies in every city, saying that chains and tribulations await me. But none of these things move me, nor do I count my life dear to myself, so that I may finish my race with joy, and the ministry which I received from the Lord Jesus, to testify to the gospel of the grace of God" (Acts 20:24).

"And now I know that you all, among whom I have gone preaching the kingdom of God, will see my face no more.

"Take heed therefore to yourselves and to all the flock, among which the Holy Spirit has made you overseers, to shepherd the church of God which He purchased with His own blood," he counseled the elders. "For I know this, that after I leave, savage wolves will come in among you, and will not spare the flock.

"For three years I did not cease to warn everyone night and day with tears. Now, brethren, I commend you to God and to the word of His grace, which is able to build you up and give you an inheritance among all those who are sanctified [separated and dedicated to God].... I have shown you in every way, in laboring like this, that you must support the weak" (Acts 20).

As Paul knelt and prayed with the men, they wept freely, fell on his neck, and kissed him, sorrowing most of all that they would not see his face again. They accompanied him to the ship.

Ruins of Celsus Library in Ephesus. (Photo by Jordan Rosa, Ensign, US Navy, from Gainesville, Florida) Long languishing in ruin, Ephesus is now undergoing major restoration. Great effort is being devoted to excavating this almost five-thousand-year-old site, including ruins of the Library of Celsus on Curates Street (above), where Paul once walked. In 2012, government officials in Turkey approved a plan to reconstruct parts of the ancient city. The library is one of the few remaining examples of an ancient Roman-influenced library.

CHAPTER 15

PREACHING RESURRECTION POWER LANDS PAUL IN PRISON AGAIN

Paul sailed to a variety of cities before unloading cargo in the Phoenician city of Tyre on the Mediterranean coast of southern Lebanon. He stayed a week with a group of disciples who warned him not to go to Jerusalem, but he and his traveling companions continued on to Caesarea and stayed many days in the home of Philip the evangelist. While there, a prophet named Agabus came from Judea and gave Paul a warning that he said came from the Holy Spirit: the Jews in Jerusalem would arrest him and deliver him to the Gentiles. Paul's traveling friends, including Luke the evangelist, begged him not to go to Jerusalem.

"What do you mean by weeping and breaking my heart?" he responded. "For I am ready not only to be bound, but also to die in Jerusalem for the name of the Lord Jesus" (Acts 21:13).

His friends decided it was useless to try changing Paul's mind. They accompanied him to Jerusalem, along with some of the disciples from Caesarea and an early disciple from Cyprus, with whom they would lodge. Paul went with the group to see James and the elders, and informed them of the major conversions to Christ among the Gentiles. Those who heard the report praised God but also cautioned Paul, "The Jews have heard you teach all the Jews who are among the Gentiles to forsake Moses, saying that they ought not to circumcise their children nor to walk according to the customs" (Acts 21:21).

Heeding his friends' advice, Paul joined them in the ceremonial Jewish ablution (required washing) before entering the temple, where he announced the end of the days of cleansing. The seven days were almost ended when, tragically, the prophesy of the Holy Spirit (through Agabus) became reality. A fierce riot broke out as Jews from the province of Asia saw Paul in the temple and dragged him out on charges of bringing Gentiles past the boundary that marked the sacred area reserved only for Jews. This offense carried a death penalty.

Paul was targeted by a "lynch-him" crowd on the city streets. His life was spared only when Roman officials intervened.

The commander, Claudius Lysias, took soldiers and centurions into the streets, and when the people saw this show of force, they stopped beating Paul. The commander ordered him to be bound with chains and asked who he was and what he had done. The people cried out with such conflicting charges that the commander secluded Paul in the barracks. Soldiers carried him up the steps to protect him from furious Jews, screaming, "Away with him" (Acts 21:35–36).

Paul told the commander, "I am a Jew from Tarsus in Cilicia, a citizen of no mean city, and I implore you, permit me to speak to the people" (Acts 21:39).

His request was granted, and he addressed the threatening mob in Aramaic. The rioters quieted down, and Paul sought common ground with his accusers. He informed them he was born and raised in Tarsus, studied under Dr. Gamaliel, and was taught "according to the strictness of our fathers' laws. I was just as zealous for God as any of you are today." He confessed his wretched past life of persecuting Christians to the death and told them about his unexpected midday encounter with the resurrected Jesus Christ on the road to Damascus. He recalled how he was blind for three days until his sight was restored by Ananias, a devout Christ follower, and how Christ commissioned him, in an audible voice, to present the Gospel to the Gentiles.

The Jerusalem Jews listened attentively but were not impressed by his talk of preaching to the Gentiles. They ranted, "Away with such a fellow from the earth, for he is not fit to live." They shouted, tore off their clothes, and threw dust into the air. The commander ordered Paul to be taken into the barracks and examined under extreme heavy beating to force him to say more about what he had done that prompted the Jews to seek his death.

As they bound him with thongs, Paul, who was sorely seasoned in pain and harsh trials, asked the centurion standing nearby, "Is it lawful for you to scourge a man who is a Roman and not condemned?" (His Roman citizenship secured him immunity from shameful punishment and granted him the right to a fair trial.)

Quickly, the centurion advised Lysias, the commander, "Take care what you do, for this man is a Roman" (Acts 22:26).

Lysias asked Paul if he really was a Roman, and he said yes. The commander responded, "With a large sum I obtained this citizenship."

"But I was born a citizen," Paul said.

Without a word, the husky slave, who was to carry out the beating, laid down the heavy rawhide whips tipped with jagged bits of zinc, iron, and bone. Paul was taken down from the beam where his naked body was stretched, awaiting the scourge. At least this time, Paul would suffer no flogging with the dreaded flagellum. He was released from his bonds the next day.

The commander remained anxious to know why the Jews did not believe Paul was fit to live. They had charged him with defiling the temple by allowing unconverted Gentiles to enter it, with teachings that in many points contradicted the laws of Moses, and with inciting unrest among all Jews of the civilized world. He called an emergency meeting of the full Sanhedrin to hear Paul speak for himself.

Paul barely got past his introductory statement: "My brothers, I am a Pharisee descended from Pharisees. I stand on trial because of the hope of the resurrection of the dead."

The word *resurrection* was enough to set off an uproar between the Sadducees, who considered resurrection impossible, and the Pharisees, who believed in the resurrection as well as in angels and spirits. Some of the Pharisees, who were teachers of the law, did not find Paul guilty of any offense deserving punishment. But the protestors became so violent that the commander feared Paul would be torn to pieces. He seized him and secluded him in the citadel.

The next night, Paul experienced an incredibly encouraging vision in which the Lord stood by him and said, ***"Be of good cheer, Paul; for as you have testified for me in Jerusalem, so you must also bear witness at Rome"*** (Acts 23:11).

Paul was intrepid, steady, resolute, constantly aware of the powerful Spirit within him, and bolstered by God's assurances in the vision. At the very time he heard the message of hope from Christ, opposition was rising. On the streets, more than forty furious Jews had vowed with an oath not to eat or drink until they had killed Paul. They appealed to the chief priest and elders to join the Sanhedrin in petitioning the commander to bring him before them again on the pretext of seeking more accurate information about his case. They planned to ambush and kill him.

Fortunately, the son of Paul's sister heard of the plot, went into the barracks, and informed his uncle. Then Paul asked one of the centurions to take the young man to Lysias, the commander, to let him know what was happening. As events unfolded, the young man informed the commander, who warned him not to tell anyone else what he had reported. The commander, determined to save Paul, gave orders to two centurions: "Get ready a detachment of 200 soldiers, 70 horsemen and 200 spearmen to go to Caesarea at nine tonight. Provide horses for Paul so that he may be taken safely to Governor Felix" (Acts 23:24 NIV).

The military regiment led Paul under cover of darkness as far as Antipatris, at the end of the Judean hill country, then returned to the barracks while letting the cavalry go on to Caesarea, Maritima, on the Mediterranean shore. There Paul was turned over to the governor, Marcus Antonius Felix, the successor to Pontius Pilate, who promised to hear his case once his accusers arrived. He held Paul in light custody in the palace built by Herod the Great, allowing him the freedom to receive visitors.

The high priest Ananias traveled to Caesarea with some of the elders and a lawyer named Tertullus to present Paul's case to Felix. They charged him as a troublemaker who stirred up riots among the Jews and as a ringleader of the Nazarene sect, who even desecrated the temple, a capital punishment. Felix motioned for Paul to speak, and he took his place before the Sanhedrin:

"I know that for a number of years you have been a judge over this nation, so I gladly make my defense. You can easily verify that no more than twelve days ago I went up to Jerusalem to worship. My accusers did not find me arguing with anyone at the temple, or stirring up a crowd in the synagogues or anywhere else in the city. And they cannot prove to you the charges they are now making against me.

"However, I admit that I worship the God of our ancestors as a follower of the Way, which they call a sect. I believe everything that is in accordance with the Law and that is written in the Prophets, and I have the same hope in God as these men themselves have, that there will be a resurrection of both the righteous and the wicked. So I strive always to keep my conscience clear before God and man.

"After an absence of several years, I came to Jerusalem to bring my people gifts for the poor and to present offerings. I was ceremonially clean when they found me in the temple courts doing this. There was no crowd with me, nor was I involved in any disturbance. But there are some Jews from the province of Asia, who ought to be here before you and bring charges if they have anything against me. Or these who are here should state what crime they found in me when I stood before the Sanhedrin—unless it was this one thing I shouted as I stood in their presence: 'It is concerning the resurrection of the dead that I am on trial before you today'" (Acts 24:17–21 NIV).

Felix had a history of violence, greed, corruption, and cruelty as governor, so vicious that Tacitus, Rome's preeminent historian, said, "He exercised the power of a king with the mind of a slave." He adjourned the proceedings and said he would decide the case once Lysias, the commander, arrived. Meanwhile, he ordered the centurion to keep Paul under guard, with freedom for his friends to visit and take care of his needs.

On the surface, the situation appeared to be going well for Paul, but not. Felix had at some point become well acquainted with the way of Christ. When he and his Jewish wife Drusilla visited Paul privately and heard him speak about righteousness and God's final judgment to come, Felix trembled in fear for his future. He apparently aimed to pacify the Jews by leaving Paul in jail, an imprisonment that lasted two years from the time Felix himself died in office in AD 60 and Porcius Festus succeeded him as governor. Festus was in Jerusalem when Jewish leaders presented him with the charges against Paul and asked him to summon the prisoner from Caesarea. Once again, the conspirators planned to kill Paul along the way.

Governor Festus decided to convene his court in Caesarea and see Paul there. And Paul declared to Festus he had done nothing wrong against the Jewish law or against the temple or against Caesar. Festus asked if he would be willing to stand trial before him in Jerusalem.

"I am now standing before Caesar's court where I ought to be tried," Paul responded. "I have not done any wrong to the Jews, as you yourself know very well. If, however, I am guilty of doing anything deserving death, I do not refuse to die. But if the charges against me by these Jews are not true, no one has the right to hand me over to them. I appeal to Caesar!"

Festus conferred with his council and announced his decision: "You have appealed to Caesar? To Caesar you will go" (Acts 25:12).

Nothing about Paul's future would go in a straight line, despite the Lord's assurance that he would preach in Rome. King Agrippa II and his sister, Queen Bernice, arrived in Caesarea on a state visit to pay respects to Festus, and while there, Festus told him about Paul, whom the chief priests and elders of the Jews asked to be condemned. Festus explained how he had convened court and heard Paul's defense and found nothing about him deserving of death. But when Paul asked to be held until the emperor could adjudicate his case, he decided to keep him in custody until the right time to send him to Caesar.

Agrippa told Festus he wanted to hear from the prisoner himself, and his chance came the very next day before an assembly of high-ranking military officers and prominent men of the city, most of them Gentile. The king and queen arrived dressed in regal purple robes with gold circlets on their brows as crowns. The defendant was led into the courtroom in a prison tunic, his chains clinking. Paul was gaunt and scarred, but he spoke with strong resonance. His articulate defense prompted the king to think differently about Jesus the Christ, to the point he was bothered by new questions.

Paul Tells Agrippa that Prophets Predicted the Coming of Jesus

"You have permission to speak for yourself," the king said to Paul (Acts 26).

"King Agrippa, I consider myself fortunate to stand before you today as I make my defense against all the accusations of the Jews, and especially so because you are well acquainted with all the Jewish customs and controversies. Therefore, I beg you to listen to me patiently.

"The Jewish people all know the way I have lived ever since I was a child, from the beginning of my life in my own country, and also in Jerusalem. They have known me for a long time and can testify, if they are willing, that I conformed to the strictest sect of our religion, living as a Pharisee. And now it is because of my hope in what God has promised our ancestors that I am on trial today.

"This is the promise our twelve tribes [of Israel] are hoping to see fulfilled as they earnestly serve God day and night. King Agrippa, it is because of this hope that these Jews are accusing me. Why should any of you consider it incredible that God raises the dead? I too was convinced that I ought to do all that was possible to oppose the name of Jesus of Nazareth. And that is just what I did in Jerusalem. On the authority of the chief priests, I put many of the Lord's people in prison, and when they were put to death, I cast my vote against them.

"Many a time I went from one synagogue to another to have them punished, and I tried to force them to blaspheme. I was so obsessed with persecuting them that I even hunted them down in foreign cities" (Acts 26:11 NIV).

Paul shared with the king how he met the resurrected Christ on the road to Damascus and heard Jesus say, ***"I am sending you to them [the Gentiles] to open their eyes and turn them from darkness to light, and from the power of Satan to God, so that they may receive forgiveness of their sins and a place among those who are sanctified by faith in me"*** (Acts 26:18 NIV).

"So then, King Agrippa, I was not disobedient to the vision from heaven. First to those in Damascus, then to those in Jerusalem and in all Judea, and then to the Gentiles, I preached that they should repent and turn to God and demonstrate their repentance by their deeds. That is why some Jews seized me in the temple courts and tried to kill me. But God has helped me to this very day; so I stand here and testify to small and great alike. I am saying nothing beyond what the prophets and Moses said would happen ... that the Messiah would suffer and, as the first to rise from the dead, would bring the message of light to his own people and to the Gentiles" (Acts 26:19–23 NIV).

At this point, Festus interrupted, "You are out of your mind, Paul! Your great learning is driving you insane."

"I am not insane, most excellent Festus," Paul asserted. "What I am saying is true and reasonable. The king is familiar with these things, and I can speak freely to him. I am convinced that none of this has escaped his notice, because it was not done in a corner. King Agrippa, do you believe the prophets? I know you do."

Agrippa then said to Paul, "Do you think that in such a short time you can persuade me to be a Christian?"

"Short time or long—I pray to God that not only you, but all who are listening to me today may become what I am, except for these chains," Paul replied (Acts 26:29 NIV).

The king rose to his feet, along with the governor, Queen Bernice, and those sitting with them. After they left, they began saying that this man was not doing anything that deserved death or imprisonment.

Agrippa said to Festus, "This man could have been set free if he had not appealed to Caesar."

A decision was made for Paul and some other prisoners to be handed over to a centurion named Julius, captain of the Imperial Regiment. They embarked in a ship from Adramyttium in Aeolis in modern-day Turkey, and later, Julius found an Alexandrian grain freighter sailing for Italy (Acts 27:6). At last, Paul was on his way to Rome, although he had not expected to go as a political prisoner.

The repeated threats against Paul's life leading to his imprisonment in Caesarea naturally trigger the question of how he could stay the course when he knew his future involved more of the same. Answers lie not only in scripture, but in modern-day parallels of Christians serving God in the face of adversaries as threatening as devouring lions.

David Platt, pastor of McLean Baptist Church in suburban Virginia, wrote about such threats in his best-selling book, *Radical: Taking Back Your Faith from the American Dream.* In the opening pages, he takes the reader to an unnamed country in Asia, where a group of Christian church leaders were meeting secretly, an illegal act. People caught doing so could lose their land, their jobs, their families, or their lives. Platt recalls the meeting:

> Imagine all the blinds closed on the windows of a dimly lit room. Twenty leaders from different churches in the area sat in a circle on the floor with their Bibles open. Some of them had sweat on their foreheads after walking for miles to get there. Others were dirty from the dust in the villages from which they had set out on bikes early that morning.
>
> I listened as they began sharing stories of what God was doing in their churches.
>
> One man sat in the corner. He had a strong frame, and he served as the head of security, so to speak. Whenever a knock was heard at the door or a noise was made outside the window, everyone in the room would freeze in tension as this brother would go to make sure everything was okay. As he spoke, his rough appearance soon revealed a tender heart.
>
> "Some of the people in my church have been pulled away by a cult," he said, referring to a cult known for kidnapping and torturing believers. As he shared

about the dangers his church members were facing, tears welled up in his eyes.

"I am hurting," he said, "and I need God's grace to lead my church through these attacks."

A woman on the other side of the room spoke up next. "Some of the members in my church were recently confronted by government officials."

She continued, "They threatened their families, saying that if they did not stop gathering to study the Bible, they were going to lose everything they had."

She asked for prayers, saying, "I need to know how to lead my church to follow Christ even when it costs them everything."

As I looked around the room, I saw that everyone was now in tears. The struggles expressed by this brother and sister were not isolated. They all looked at one another and said, "We need to pray." Immediately they went to their knees, and with their faces on the ground, they began to cry out to God.

Their prayers were marked less by grandiose theological language and more by heart-felt praise and pleading.

"O God, thank you for loving us."

"O God, we need you."

"Jesus, we give our lives to you and for you."

They wept before God as one leader after another prayed. After about an hour, the room drew to a silence, and they rose from the floor. Humbled by

> what I had just been a part of, I saw puddles of tears in a circle around the room.

Platt, who is a nondenominational Christian, wrote that since then, God has granted him many other opportunities to meet with believers in underground churches in Asia, where men and women are risking everything to follow Christ.

From the Pen of Paul

Walk in the Holy Spirit

There is now no condemnation to those who are in Christ Jesus, who do not walk according to the flesh, but according to the Spirit. For the law of the Spirit of life in Christ Jesus has made me free from the law of sin and death.

For what the law could not do in that it was weak through the flesh, God did by sending His own Son in the likeness of sinful flesh, on account of sin. He condemned sin in the flesh, that the righteous requirement of the law might be fulfilled in us who do not walk according to the flesh, but according to the Spirit.

For those who live according to the flesh set their minds on the things of the flesh, but those who live according to the Spirit, the things of the Spirit.

For to be carnally minded is death, but to be spiritually minded is life and peace. (Romans 8:1–6)

CHAPTER 16

ISLAND NATION OF MALTA TRANSFORMED BY THE GOSPEL

Through a monstrous storm that wrecked his ship on the rocky shoals of Malta in the middle of the Mediterranean Sea, Paul brought Christianity to the Roman island colony in about AD 60.

He was aboard the ship as a prisoner of Rome, charged with inciting the Jews against Roman authority. He was part of a shipload of 276 people headed for the world capital, where he was slated to appeal his imprisonment to the emperor, Claudius Caesar Nero. As a Roman citizen born in Tarsus, he had the right to present his plea at the highest level.

Paul clung to a slim chance that he could win his appeal. He wore loose chains and was guarded by Roman soldiers as he boarded the grain freighter commissioned by Julius. They departed from a port in Caesarea. The huge ship featured a single wooden mast, a bird's head carving above the bows, and a bird's tail at the stern. It was part of a special fleet designed and constructed by the Romans expressly to transport grain from the fertile land of the Nile to Italy, particularly to Rome.

The guards risked severe punishment if they failed to keep the prisoners secured, but no one at the time worried about the prisoners when a rip-roaring Euroclydon (a typhonic wind) blew the freighter off course and into dark turbulence. The storm hit as the freighter was sailing along the coast of Crete. The sea churned furiously, and the stout timbers cracked and buckled. Glassy-eyed men stumbled as they slid across the slippery, heaving deck. They screamed useless commands as the waves soared over their heads; the raging wind made it impossible to steer.

Thick, dark, unbroken clouds blocked out the sun and stars. The captain had no compass or chronometer and only a rough chart and primitive form of quadrant. Without seeing the sun or stars to take a bearing, he had no way to determine the ship's position.

As the ship shuddered and sank deeper in the sea, the cargo of Egyptian wheat, an important asset in the Roman economy, became waterlogged and very heavy. On the third day, the crew threw overboard the ship's tackle and cables used to reinforce the hull.

The storm was far from over; it would last another eleven days, and the bedraggled travelers were losing hope that they would live through it. They realized it would be impossible to tack back to Fair Havens harbor near the city of Lasea, which they had just left. While the howling winter wind tossed the vessel as if it were cork, Paul stood hobbled in his iron shackles and admonished the sailors for not listening to his earlier warnings not to sail from Crete and risk this catastrophe.

But in an abrupt softening of tone, the balding, gray-bearded apostle spoke to the people hunkered down near him, bleary-eyed and grasping for anything solid to hold onto. He was too stooped from repeated beatings and tormenting imprisonment to stand straight, but given the inner strength of the Spirit, his voice carried clearly above the shattering roar:

"I urge you to take heart for there will be no loss of life among you, but only of the ship! For there stood by me this night an angel of the God to whom I belong and whom I serve, saying 'Do not be afraid, Paul; you must be brought before Caesar, and indeed God has granted you all those who sail with you.' Therefore, take heart, men, for I believe God that it will be just as it was told me. However, we must run aground on a certain island."

At near midnight on the fourteenth night, sensing that they might be drawing close to land, the sailors took soundings and calculated the seabed was 120 feet deep. A short time later, they took soundings again and found it was ninety feet deep. Afraid they might be grounded on rocks, they cut loose four massive lead and wood anchors, let them drop through the hawse holes in the bow of the ship, and watched them disappear in the ocean. They hoisted the lifeboat onto the deck, loosened the rudder ropes, unfurled the foresail to the wind, and headed for shore.

At daybreak, Paul prayed thanks to God and ate a piece of moldy bread. He urged everyone to do the same, for they had gone fourteen days with little or no food. "This is your survival," he said.

After everyone had eaten some of the bread, sailors lightened the ship by heaving overboard the sodden sacks of grain. The ship twisted in the savage wind and began to break apart. At a place "where two seas meet," the crew ran the freighter aground. The prow stuck fast and remained immovable, and the stern was broken up by the breakers. The ship was a total loss.

All escaped safely to land, but none of them recognized where they were. The Roman soldiers had planned to kill Paul and the other prisoners under their guard to prevent them swimming away and escaping, but Julius, the centurion, aimed to spare Paul's life (Acts 27:42). He commanded those who could swim to jump overboard and find their way to solid ground.

In the rain on a chilly late August day, the rest of the exhausted passengers and crew, including some women and children, left the wreckage and slogged through the mud on shaky legs to reach firmer ground on shore. Some paddled the last few yards on pieces of the wreckage. They were ragged and cold and haunted by their brush with death. But despair was erased as they were welcomed in an extraordinary way by friendly natives. In keeping with their tradition of hospitality, the islanders kindled a bonfire and motioned for the exhausted castaways to come warm themselves.

Paul the convict, who had worked as hard as the seasoned sailors to save the ship, was gathering brushwood for the fire when a snake, obviously seeking to escape the heat, fastened itself to his hand (Acts 28:3).

A crowd of Maltese, most of them descendants of Phoenicians who spoke only their Punic dialect, stared wide-eyed at the viper dangling from Paul's hand until he shook it off into the fire. If they had wanted to tell him the snake was venomous, they did not know how to say it in Greek or Hebrew. Having heard that prisoners were aboard the ship, they said to one another, "No doubt this man is a murderer ... he has escaped the sea, yet justice does not allow [him] to live" (Acts 18:4).

The people expected Paul to swell up or fall dead and that their goddess of justice would make sure he reaped the consequences for whatever evil they perceived he had committed. But after a long watch, seeing that he showed no ill effects, they decided he must be a god.

Sunrise must have been blissful for the tattered survivors when they awoke to find themselves warm and dry, surrounded by kind folk who called this place home. The mist lifted, and light flickered across the stony cliffs, the beautiful sandy beaches, and the balmy blue-green sea.

Victory of a different order lay just ahead for Paul, who stayed several days as a guest in the estate home of Publius, the Roman governor of the island. Hearing that the governor's father was deathly ill with fever and dysentery, Paul went to his bedside, laid his hands on the man, and prayed in the name of Jesus, and he was healed. Word of this event spread rapidly across the small island. Publius, who had blessed Paul with his generous hospitality, was soon to be blessed for doing so.

Paul was no doubt caught by surprise when men, women, and children, suffering a variety of illnesses, came to ask him to touch them. He repeatedly placed his hands on them and prayed for their recovery. As Luke described the scene in Acts 28:9, all of them were cured. He became a devoted friend to the Maltese, and they took him under their wings, assuring his comfort.

Publius's father converted to Christianity, and soon hundreds of other locals, who had worshipped idols, also claimed faith in Jesus, the risen Son of God, to whom Paul prayed.

Later, the established Roman Catholic Church named him the first bishop of Malta. The influence of Christianity in Malta has continued through the centuries. According to Freedom House and the World Factbook, some 98 percent of people in the Maltese Republic adhere to Roman Catholicism.

Details of the harrowing Malta shipwreck, from descriptions of the grain freighter to the exact depth of the seabed from two different soundings and a track of the ship route, reflect the careful journalism of Luke, the evangelist and Greek physician, a disciple of Paul, who was with him on this voyage. Luke's descriptions of the wind, sea, and coast during the disastrous voyage (Acts 27–28) were verified in the mid-nineteenth century when Paul's route was retraced by a Scot named James Smith.

During the three winter months in Malta, Paul worked as a laborer and as a minister who healed the sick. Spring arrived, and the wind changed so that he and his fellow voyagers could sail northward to Italy. When the time came for Paul to be transferred to Rome for trial, the island people showered him, Aristarchus, and Luke with supplies and gifts. They presented them with an Alexandrian ship with a carved figurehead of the twin mythical Greek gods Castor and Pollux, who were worshipped as sons of Zeus and believed to assure safety in the sea. Paul and his companions boarded the ship for Rome on a spring day, when the sea was tranquil.

Saint Paul is memorialized across the island, especially at Saint Paul's Bay, where tourists visit the Church of St. Paul's Shipwreck, a Roman Catholic parish church in the capital city of Valletta.

An Electrifying Discovery

Four huge ancient Roman-era anchors of the type described in the biblical story of Apostle Paul's shipwreck on the Island of Malta were dug up sometime in the early 1960s (the date was not remembered by the man who discovered them). Ray Ciancio was simply excited at the time to have found big pieces of lead. But he later explained the finding to Bob Cornuke, a former Los Angeles crime scene investigator, who was trying to find the lost anchors by tracking information found in the Bible.

Cornuke discovered that the place where the anchors were retrieved matched Luke's descriptions in Acts 27-28. The anchors were later donated to the National Maritime Museum, and expert analysis confirmed they were Roman-era anchors from the right time period.

Today, the anchors are tucked away in a corner of Valletta's Maritime Museum, labeled simply "Roman Anchors."

CHAPTER 17

AMBASSADOR IN CHAINS SHARES LOVE OF CHRIST IN ROME

In AD 60, Paul arrived in Rome, the vibrant capital city of two or three million people and center of influence in the vast Roman Empire. God had reassured him in a vision that he would preach here, but he had not expected to arrive chained to a Roman soldier.

Paul, the apostle commissioned by Jesus Christ in a heavenly vision, was elated by the prospect of sharing the Gospel of love and redemption with a huge population of Gentiles, along with fifty thousand Jews. But he was on house arrest, held in custody in a rental dwelling. Although vastly better than being secluded in prison, he would have no speaker's stage, no amphitheater, no marketplace forum, no hilltop or elevated platform as in a synagogue.

The limitations might have stymied a less determined ambassador, but Paul opened a home church, inviting all who would come, and proved his pen mightier than a podium. He preached and wrote some of what he preached in letters to previously established churches. In fact, during his house arrest, he finished the letters (New Testament books) to the Ephesians, the Philippians, the Colossians, and Philemon. In his highly revered Letter to the Romans, written in Corinth well ahead of his arrival in the city, he referred to himself as a bondservant of Jesus Christ, highlighting the fact he had been bought with a price through Christ's sacrificial death and therefore was "owned" by Him.

Who would listen to a prisoner in chains accused of blasphemy against Rome?

Paul would answer the question by inviting house guests, starting with two meetings with Rome's leading Jews, noted in Acts 28. He made sure they understood that he held no grievance against his own people, the Jews.

"My brothers," he said to them. "Although I have done nothing against our people or against the customs of our ancestors, I was arrested in Jerusalem and handed over to the Romans. They examined me and wanted to release me because I was not guilty of any crime deserving death. The Jews objected, so I was compelled to make an appeal to Caesar. I certainly did not intend to bring any charge against my own people.

"For this reason, I have asked to see you and talk with you. It is because of the hope of Israel that I am bound with this chain" (Acts 28:20 NIV).

The Jewish visitors told Paul they had received no negative reports about him, but they wanted to hear his views regarding this sect (Christianity) that people everywhere were talking about. A larger group of Jews came to Paul's place for another meeting where he engaged in lengthy conversation, from morning to evening, about Jesus Christ and the Kingdom of God. Some of the Jewish authorities stubbornly rejected his message, while others were persuaded by the Gospel he proclaimed (Acts 28:24).

He shared with them words that the Holy Spirit spoke through Isaiah the prophet: ***"Go to this people and say, 'Hearing you will hear and shall not understand, and seeing you will see and not perceive, for the hearts of this people have grown dull. Their ears are hard of hearing and their eyes they have closed, lest they should see with their eyes and hear with their ears, lest they should understand with their hearts and turn, so that I should heal them."*** (Acts 28:25–27)

"Therefore, I want you to know that God's salvation has been sent to the Gentiles, and they will listen" (Acts 28:28 NIV).

Many people began to hear about Paul's ministry and found their way to his house. The book of Romans does not identify the visitors who became converts to Christianity, but one of them is detailed in the brief book of Philemon. The story is of an escaped slave named Onesimus, owned by Philemon, a landowner in the city of Colossae, also known to Paul as the director of a home church. Onesimus had run away from Colossae to Rome, probably hoping to lose himself in that crowded metropolis. He may have stolen money from his owner, but the Bible does not make this clear. Providentially, he met Paul, who shared the Gospel with him and influenced him to declare faith in Christ.

Onesimus made himself useful to Paul and earned his respect, to the point that Paul began to call him "my child." Roman law required that Paul return Onesimus to his master, with serious penalties if he failed to do so. But Paul went beyond legal rule. He wrote a letter to Philemon, praising him for his loving encouragements in the past and explaining how Onesimus had found his way to his house and had decided to become a Christian. He told Philemon how Onesimus had proven himself to be a great helper. He then appealed to him to receive him not as a slave but as a dear brother.

"He became a son while I was in chains," Paul wrote. "I am sending him, who is my very heart, back to you. Formerly, he was useless to you, but now he has become useful both to you and to me. I am sending him, who is my very heart, back to you.... So, if you consider me a partner, welcome him as you would welcome me" (Philippians 1:12 NIV).

The story gives insight into how Paul sought to undermine slavery by placing the relationship between slave and owner under the banner of love rather than commerce. He wrote to Philemon in his own handwriting, "If he has done you any wrong or owes you anything, charge it to me."

Paul's actions reflect his conviction that God gives equal esteem to Jew and Gentile, male and female, bond (servant) and free (Galatians 3:28). For unknown reasons, he chose not to conduct a frontal assault against the culturally entrenched, multilayered system of slavery, but he demonstrated the compassionate love of Christ for all people and the indwelling Spirit of God.

Paul Preaches Stunning Message: Man Is Saved by Grace, Not Works

"The just [righteous] shall live by faith," Paul wrote in the opening chapter of Romans. And later in the same book, "We conclude that a man is justified by faith apart from the deeds of the law" (Romans 3:28).

Paul shook up the religious world of his day by preaching that Christ's plan of salvation has nothing to do with earning God's favor through good deeds. He had no way of knowing that a little over fifteen hundred years after he made these statements, Martin Luther, a young Augustinian monk and professor of theology serving Pope Leo X in Wittenberg, Germany, would read "the just shall live by faith" in his Greek-Latin New Testament. He read the words again and again, and realized the Roman Catholic Church, the ruling church of the day, was misinterpreting scripture and teaching false doctrine. While in his early thirties, he began a bitter and unrelenting dispute with the church regarding its inaccurate theology, especially in regard to salvation.

Luther was seeking salvation in the rites and ideology of the Catholic Church—one that says church tradition and scripture must be honored with equal devotion—and he feared he would never win God's approval. He might just as well have been smitten by Jesus's promise: ***"God so loved the world that He gave His only begotten Son that whoever believes in Him shall not perish, but have everlasting life"*** (John 3:16). But it happened that the short sentence in Romans ("the just shall live by faith") reached Luther's conscience, touched his heart, and led him to launch a courageous protest, which led to the sixteenth-century Protestant Reformation.

Luther had not planned a fight. He aimed to awaken the ruling church and everyone else to the truth in God's word. The biblical doctrine that he championed, called *solo fide*, or "justification by faith alone," continues to distinguish most Protestant Christian churches from the Roman Catholic Church, as well as the Eastern Orthodox churches and Oriental Orthodox churches.

His teaching represented a radical departure from Roman Catholic teaching that faithfulness to the rituals and practices of the church help a person earn God's salvation. He was excommunicated by the church when he openly opposed its practice of selling indulgences (papers signed by the pope to pardon a person from sin). He was out of the church but no longer safe. He went into hiding for about ten months at Wartburg Castle near Eisenach, to elude church authorities determined to kill him. While there, he busied himself translating the New Testament from its original Koine Greek, the original Alexandrian dialect or biblical Greek, into German so that the common people could understand it.

Luther wrote the song that became the battle hymn of the Reformation: "A Mighty Fortress Is Our God" (*Ein feste Burg ist unser Gott*), which ends with the stirring challenge, "Let goods and kindred go, this mortal life also; the body they may kill, God's truth abideth still—His kingdom is forever" (the words are a paraphrase of Psalm 46).

The sale of indulgences, which helped pay for the lavish St. Peter's Basilica in Vatican City (the largest church in the world), was outlawed by the Roman Catholic Church in 1567. The church has, in print, referred to this practice as an obvious corruption of the doctrine. However, Catholic churches have recently revived the practice of indulgences and have not renounced them as non-biblical.

Today, charitable gifts to the church, along with good deeds or acts of penance assigned by the church, can help people earn an indulgence, which can allegedly lessen the punishment ultimately received for their sins. Catholics draw from the church's Treasury of Merits, which is like a spiritual storehouse of excess merits and virtues of all Catholic saints, including the Virgin Mary and the sinless Jesus Christ. In fact, if Catholics sin, they can gain the forgiveness of God by seeking to apply to their credit the good life of someone else (Source: article by Mike T. Rogacs in *Truth Magazine*, February 2019).

Luther became a prolific Christian writer, with extensive focus on the work of the Holy Spirit to sanctify believers; that is, to help them become holy. Here are a few excerpts from his articles:

> The believing man has the Holy Ghost [Spirit], and where the Holy Spirit dwells, He will not suffer a man to be idle, but stirs him up to all exercises of piety and godliness, and of true religion, to the love of God, to the patient suffering of afflictions, to prayer, to thanksgiving, and the exercise of charity toward all men.
>
> The heart overflows with gladness, and leaps and dances for the joy it has found in God. In this experience the Holy Spirit is active, and has taught us in the flash of a moment the deep secret of joy. You will have as much joy and laughter in life as you have faith in God.

> Faith is a living, bold trust in God's grace, so certain of God's favor that it would risk death a thousand times trusting in it. Such confidence and knowledge of God's grace makes you happy, joyful and bold in your relationship to God and all creatures. The Holy Spirit makes this happen through faith. Because of it, you freely, willingly and joyfully do good to everyone, serve everyone, suffer all kinds of things, love and praise the God who has shown you such grace.

Bible Translator Tyndale Distinguishes the Law and the Gospel

During the time of the Protestant Reformation, William Tyndale, an English scholar known for translating the Bible into English, described the law and the Gospel as two keys. He said the law is the key that shuts up all men under condemnation, while the Gospel is the key that opens the door and lets them out. In such a short statement, Tyndale defined the difference between God's Old Covenant, based on the laws He gave to Moses, and the New Covenant, which frees believers from a legalistic religion and bases salvation on faith in Christ alone.

In the words of Apostle Paul, no one will be justified in God's sight by the deeds of the law. He wrote in Romans 3:23, "All have sinned and fall short of the glory of God, being justified freely by His grace [God's mercy] through the redemption that is in Jesus Christ."

"Therefore, having been justified by faith, we have peace with God through our Lord Jesus Christ, through whom we also have access by faith into this grace in which we stand, and rejoice in hope of the glory of God. Not only that, but we also glory in tribulations, knowing that tribulation produces perseverance; and perseverance, character; and character, hope. Now hope does not disappoint, because the love of God has been poured out in our hearts by the Holy Spirit who was given to us" (Romans 5:1–5).

Paul said the "old man," meaning the former self-focused person before God's merciful forgiveness is nothing like the new life in Christ. He preached that all who believe and are baptized in the name of Jesus are to reckon themselves "dead to sin and alive to God in Christ Jesus, forbidding sin to reign in their mortal bodies." He stressed, "Now having been set free from sin and having become slaves of God, you have your fruit to holiness, and in the end, everlasting life. For the wages of sin is death, but the gift of God is eternal life in Christ Jesus our Lord" (Romans 6:23).

Paul shared with the Galatians the fact that as he drew increasingly close to Christ, he became less conscious of himself and was subsumed by His holy living presence within.

"Through the law I died to the law so that I might live for God. I have been crucified with Christ and I no longer live, but Christ lives in me. I live by faith in the Son of God who loved me and gave himself for me" (Galatians 2:19–20).

"There is therefore no condemnation to those who are in Christ Jesus, who do not walk according to the flesh, but according to the Spirit. For the law of the Spirit of life in Christ Jesus has made me free from the law of sin and death.... For those who live according to the flesh set their minds on the things of the flesh, but those who live according to the Spirit, the things of the Spirit. For to be carnally minded is death, but to be spiritually minded is life and peace" (Romans 8:1–6).

Paul asserted that laws have a weak effect in governing a person's behavior and cannot accomplish in the heart what the Spirit can do. Because of universally pervasive sin, God sent His Son in the form of human flesh to condemn sin, and those who are led by the Spirit of God become His adopted sons. And the children of God, he said, are "heirs of God and joint heirs with Christ if indeed we suffer with Him, that we may also be glorified together." A loving relationship is created between God and His adopted children, far superior to a constant struggle to meet the requirements of law.

From his fixed location, under constant watch by a soldier from the prestigious Praetorian Guard, Paul could have complained he was unable to reach the Roman people, but his outreach extended far beyond his rental house. He wrote to the Philippian Christians, "Brethren, the things which happened to me have actually turned out for the furtherance of the gospel, so that it has become evident to the whole palace guard [a body of ten thousand privileged troops appointed by Augustus] and to all the rest, that my chains are in Christ."

The Gospel, apparently in connection with Paul's ministry, had penetrated the royal palace and won converts there. These converts had free communication with the apostle, and he with them. Paul said the Roman Christians had gained confidence after watching him preach while in chains and "dare all the more to proclaim the gospel without fear" (Philippians 1:14 NIV).

To his disappointment, however, certain members of the congregation, envious of Paul, began to preach Christ, not to win souls to Jesus, but to increase opposition to Paul. If anyone raised an objection to their messages, they would refer them to Paul, their leader.

Aware of the people conniving against him, Paul encouraged the sincere Christians to "rejoice in the Lord always. Let your gentleness be known to all men. The Lord is at hand. Be anxious for nothing, but in everything by prayer and supplication, with thanksgiving, let your requests be made known to God; and the peace of God, which surpasses all understanding, will guard your hearts and minds through Christ Jesus" (Philippians 4:4–7).

Out of his deep understanding of prophecy and of the mission of Christ, Paul wrote a concise definition of how a person can be saved: "If you confess with your mouth the Lord Jesus and believe in your heart that God has raised Him from the dead, you will be saved." And even shorter is his statement in Romans 10:13: "Whoever calls on the name of the Lord shall be saved."

He also taught that while "all have sinned and come short of the glory of God," justification is provided to all by the grace of God through the redemption that is in Christ Jesus.

"I beseech you therefore, brethren, by the mercies of God, that you present your bodies a living sacrifice, holy, acceptable to God, which is your reasonable service. And do not be conformed to this world, but be transformed by the renewing of your mind, that you may prove what is that good and acceptable and perfect will of God" (Romans 12:1–2).

Paul taught the new converts in Rome that they should use their spiritual gifts from God in prophecy, ministry, teaching, and helping people in need. He cautioned them not to be overcome with evil but to "overcome evil with good."

"The night is far spent, the day is at hand," he said. "Therefore, let us cast off the works of darkness, and let us put on the armor of light" (Romans 13:12).

He assured believers that when faced with overwhelming problems and crises—a loved one is injured or dying, a spouse leaves the marriage, a child is mentally disturbed, a diagnosis of stage 4 cancer—the Holy Spirit prays for the suffering person. "For we do not know what we should pray for as we ought, but the Spirit Himself makes intercession for us with groanings which cannot be uttered" (Romans 8:26).

Paul Recalls the Agonies of Near-Defeat

Paul rarely spoke of his own suffering, but one day while speaking to the church at Corinth, he recalled great dangers he had endured: an earthquake, three shipwrecks, twenty-four hours floating in the open sea, countless beatings, the "thirty-nine lashes" (the customary limit of a beating) five times, a nearly fatal stoning, losing and regaining his sight, a hasty basket ride down a city wall at night, the bite of a poisonous snake, treacherous adversaries, lengthy imprisonments, a plot by men not to eat until they killed him, and violent riots. He recalled facing perils of the Gentiles and among false brethren; perils in the city, the wilderness, and the ocean; and of times when he was bone-tired, hungry, thirsty, cold, and naked (2 Corinthians 11:23–27).

He also spoke of his periodic affliction with an unidentified, painful "thorn in the flesh" that he asked God three times to remove. His prayer was not answered, but God reassured him, ***"My grace is sufficient for you, for power is perfected in weakness,"*** and Paul felt his strength compounded (2 Corinthians 12:9). Paul said the thorn was a tormenting message from Satan designed to keep him from being conceited.

"Most gladly, therefore, I will rather boast about my weaknesses, that the power of Christ may dwell in me. Therefore, I am well content with weaknesses, with insults, with distresses, with persecutions, with difficulties, for Christ's sake, for when I am weak, then I am strong," he said.

Paul's repeated recoveries from severe physical insults indicate he was able to face mountainous problems that would crush less vigorous men. But he was a man of flesh and blood, as subject to pain as anyone, and during his ministry, he endured extremely low points. He suffered such severe tribulations and dire threats that at one point, he feared his life would soon end. He described the agony of his near-defeat and expressed the purposes of his sufferings in his second letter to the Church of God in Corinth. Note his extraordinary opening:

"Blessed be the God and Father of our Lord Jesus Christ, the Father of mercies and God of all comfort, who comforts us in all our tribulation, that we may be able to comfort those who are in any trouble, with the comfort with which we ourselves are comforted by God. For as the sufferings of Christ abound in us, so our consolation also abounds through Christ.

"We do not want you to be unaware, brethren, of our affliction which came to us in Asia, that we were burdened excessively, beyond our strength, so that we despaired even of life. Indeed, we had the sentence of death within ourselves in order that we should not trust in ourselves, but in God who raises the dead, who delivered us from so great a peril of death, and will deliver us, He on whom we have set our hope" (2 Corinthians 1:8–10).

Although hard-stricken by both natural disasters and the persecutions of men who challenged his authority as an apostle and accused him of being a wimp, Paul found the strength of the indwelling Spirit to stay his course. The words he wrote help comfort the troubled soul:

"We faint not. We are troubled on every side, yet not distressed. We are perplexed, but not in despair; persecuted but not forsaken; cast down but not destroyed; always bearing about in the body the dying of the Lord Jesus, that the life also of Jesus might be made manifest in our body" (2 Corinthians 4:1 and 8–10). We do not lose heart. Though outwardly we are wasting away, yet inwardly we are being renewed day by day. For our light and momentary troubles are achieving for us an eternal glory that far outweighs them all. We fix our eyes not on what is seen, but on what is unseen, since what is seen is temporary, but what is unseen is eternal" (2 Corinthians 4:16–18).

Paul talked openly about his inner struggles with sins that threatened to captivate him and would have done so, if not for his firm conviction that "the law of the Spirit of life in Christ Jesus has made me free from the law of sin and death." He concluded, after a lengthy confession, "For what I will to do that I do not practice, but what I hate, that I do.... For I delight in the law of God according to the inward man. But I see another law in my members warring against the law of my mind, and bringing me into captivity to the law of sin which is in my members. O wretched man that I am! Who will deliver me from this body of death?" (Romans 7).

Beyond His Afflictions, Paul Sees Eternal Weight of Glory

In the same letter, Paul explained, "Our light affliction, which is but for a moment, works for us a far more exceeding and eternal weight of glory." He looked beyond the ordeals that stalked him to think how it will be like to be accepted by God on an everlasting basis. He referred to a weight of glory that would overshadow all of his painful and frightening experiences to the point he would look back on them as "light afflictions."

Oxford scholar and renowned Christian writer C. S. Lewis was so moved by Paul's description of "the weight of glory" that he wrote an essay on the future thrill of seeing God in person and being welcomed by Him. The essay was frequently presented in person and in radio broadcasts during World War II. He focused on his persistent thought that every living person is on the wrong side of the door, unable to see what God has in store for us.

"The door on which we have been knocking all our lives will open at last," Lewis wrote. "At present we are on the outside of the world, the wrong side of the door. We discern the freshness and purity of morning, but they do not make us fresh and pure. We cannot mingle with the splendors we see. But all the leaves of the New Testament are rustling with the rumor that it will not always be so."

Lewis cautioned, "It may be possible for each [person] to think too much of his own potential glory hereafter; it is hardly possible for him to think too often or too deeply about that of his neighbor. The load, or weight, or burden of my neighbor's glory should be laid on my back, a load so heavy that only humility can carry it, and the backs of the proud will be broken."

Paul's Perpetual Message: The Holy Spirit within You

Paul wrote extensively on the contrast between dependence on God's Spirit and people left to their own instinct and imagination. He declared an individual either belongs to the people who have the Holy Spirit within, whose hearts are being transformed by God, or to those who rely merely on human effort at its best or worst.

"Those who are led by the Spirit of God are the children of God," he wrote. "For if you live according to the Spirit, you put to death the misdeeds of the body, you will live.... The Spirit you received does not make you slaves, so that you live in fear again; rather, the Spirit you received brought about your adoption to sonship" (Romans 8:14–15). "The Spirit himself testifies with our spirit that we are God's children. Now if we are children, then we are heirs—heirs of God and co-heirs with Christ if indeed we share in His suffering in order that we may also share in His glory."

In the 1700s, Paul's description of Spirit-led believers as God's children inspired the Christian reformer and revivalist John Wesley to preach that men and women can be assured they are children of God through the inner testimony of the Holy Spirit. "The sum of all this is the testimony of the Spirit is an inward impression on the souls of believers, whereby the Spirit of God directly testifies to their spirit that they are the children of God," Wesley said.

A vivid description of the Holy Spirit's personal transformation is found in Wesley's sermons on the sanctifying work of the Spirit, Who aims to turn believers into living portraits of Jesus. He said the Spirit moves us toward the completed state that will be realized in eternity. In his words, "The gift of the Holy Spirit looks full to the resurrection; for then is the life of God completed in us."

C. S. Lewis had a colorful way of expressing the impact of the Spirit in a person's life: "If we let Him—for we can prevent Him if we choose—He will make the feeblest and filthiest of us into a dazzling, radiant, immortal creature, pulsating all through with such energy and joy and wisdom and love as we cannot now imagine, a bright, stainless mirror which reflects back to God perfectly (though of course on a smaller scale) His own boundless power and delight and goodness."

Paul knew he was an adopted son of God and that he harbored the greatest power in the universe within his heart. The book of Acts ends with a statement that for two years, he welcomed guests at his rental home, where he proclaimed the Kingdom of God and taught about the Lord Jesus Christ, with all boldness and without hindrance. But at the end of those two years, he failed to gain release from Roman imprisonment. When he realized he was unlikely to win his appeal and that his life would soon be ended, he wrote a fatherly letter to Timothy, urging him, "Hold fast the pattern of sound words which you have heard from me, in faith and love which are in Christ Jesus. That good thing which was committed to you, keep by the Holy Spirit who dwells in us."

As he approached the time of his departure, Paul wrote, "I have fought the good fight, I have finished the race, I have kept the faith. There is laid up for me the crown of righteousness, which the Lord, the righteous Judge, will give to me on that Day, and not to me only, but also to all who have loved His appearing" (2 Timothy 4:7–8).

Although the Bible does not describe the end of his life, Christian church tradition maintains that he and the apostle Peter were executed in Rome at the command of Emperor Caesar Nero. Most of the apostles of Christ were slain for their faith. One exception was John, who was ordered to be sent from Ephesus to Rome, where he miraculously escaped from a cauldron of boiling oil. Near the end of the first century, John was exiled, in punishment for his faith, to the island of Patmos, a place of imprisonment. Here, while in his eighties, he experienced visions of heaven and wrote Revelation, which became the last book in the Bible. According to church tradition, he died in Ephesus at the age of ninety-three or ninety-four.

Amazingly, martyrdom energized the rapid spread of Christianity. The second-century theologian Tertullian wrote, "The blood of the martyrs is the seed of the church." The term *martyr*, first applied to apostles, came to define everyone who suffers hardship for their faith. The early Christian period before Constantine became known as the "Age of Martyrs."

Paul and Luke were the most prolific writers of the New Testament. Under the inspiration of the Holy Spirit, they wrote about their personal experiences of God's grace, which continued to bring about the redemption of lost souls.

God caught Paul on the run and stopped him in his tracks with an audible voice from heaven that called him to preach, and he never stopped until his life was extinguished. By the time he was forced to end his ministry, he had turned a small Jewish splinter group into the makings of a world religion. By 323, Christianity was the official religion of the Roman Empire. Paul himself became one of the continuing forces in the progress of Western civilization.

Out of his voluminous writings, there looms one sentence in Romans 8:11 that captures the greatest power that can be experienced by a child of God: a permanent living presence in the heart. The sentence reveals who inspired and energized his international missionary life, helping him to rise up again and again after the near-fatal attacks of his adversaries: "The Spirit of Him who raised Jesus from the dead is living in you."

The Radiant Creature God Is Making of Us

"If we let Him—for we can prevent Him if we choose—He will make the feeblest and filthiest of us into a dazzling, radiant, immortal creature, pulsating all through with such energy and joy and wisdom and love as we cannot now imagine, a bright, stainless mirror which reflects back to God perfectly (though of course on a smaller scale) His own boundless power and delight and goodness."

—C. S. Lewis

CHAPTER 18

ROMANS: THE CATHEDRAL OF THE CHRISTIAN FAITH

Paul Speaks of a Life to be Lived

Frederick Godet, a nineteenth-century Swiss Protestant theologian, may have struggled to find the best image to describe the soul-stirring beauty of God's love and grace he experienced after reading the apostle Paul's book of Romans. Godet called the book "the cathedral of the Christian faith." In his widely acclaimed two-volume *Commentary on the Epistle to the Romans*, Godet observed that every movement of revival in the history of the Christian church has been connected to the teachings set forth in Romans.

Centuries earlier, in the summer of 386, a young man wept in the backyard of a friend. He had come to realize his life of sin and rebellion against God left him empty and feeling dead, but he could not find the strength to make a final, real decision for Jesus Christ. While sitting there, he heard children playing a game, calling out to each other, "Take up and read! Take up and read!" Thinking God had a message to him in the words of the children, he picked up a scroll (apparently a copy of Paul's letters) laying nearby and read, "not in reveling and drunkenness, not in debauchery and licentiousness, not in quarreling and jealousy. But put on the Lord Jesus Christ and make no provision for the flesh, to gratify its desires."

He did not read any further; he didn't need to. Through the power of God's Word in Romans 13:13–14, Saint Augustine of Hippo gained the faith to devote his whole life to Jesus Christ at that moment. In the year 1552, the great Christian reformer Martin Luther wrote a preface to Paul's letter to the Romans in which he described it as "the purest gospel" and as "bread for the soul."

Luther wrote, "St. Paul teaches the true liturgy and makes all Christians priests, so that they may offer, not money or cattle as priests do in the Law, but their own bodies, by putting their desires to death. Next, he describes the outward conduct of Christians whose lives are governed by the Spirit; he tells how they teach, preach, rule, serve, give, suffer, love, live and act toward friend, foe and everyone. These are the works that a Christian does, for, as I have said faith is not idle."

Paul actually wrote Romans during his missionary service in Corinth, long before he was able to reach Rome. He had been warned, indirectly from the Holy Spirit, that hostile opponents awaited him in Jerusalem, and he wondered, what if he were unable to make it to Rome? He decided to write a comprehensive letter to explain the Gospel to the Roman people, in case he was unable to see them in person. A variety of Bible commentaries have estimated he wrote the letter between 53 and 58.

The central life-changing message of Romans is that God's Holy Spirit in the human heart is powerful enough to lift men and women out of the world's milieu of sin and prepare them for a good, purpose-filled life here and now, and for eternal life in God's kingdom. The Gospel is not advice to people on how to lift themselves; the Gospel is the power that lifts them up. Paul preached that the way to perfection is through the authentic love (agape) that God revealed to us in Christ because God *is* love, and we will become like Him in communion with Him.

For Paul, the power to live a life that pleases God does not come from a person's finite ability in isolation from God, but by the power of the Holy Spirit. When he contrasts Spirit and flesh in Romans 4, he is not contrasting two aspects of human personality; he is contrasting people who are dependent on God's Spirit with those living freely to pursue their own goals.

He defined the path to salvation in simple terms: "If you confess with your mouth the Lord Jesus and believe in your heart that God has raised Him from the dead, you will be saved. For with the heart one believes unto righteousness, and with the mouth confession is made unto salvation. For the scripture says, 'Whoever believes on Him will not be put to shame.' For there is no distinction between Jew and Greek, for the same Lord over all is rich to all who call upon Him. For 'whoever calls on the name of the Lord shall be saved'" (Romans 10:9–13).

"I beseech you therefore, brethren, by the mercies of God, that you present your bodies a living sacrifice, holy, acceptable to God, which is your reasonable service. And do not be conformed to this world, but be transformed by the renewing of your mind, that you may prove what is that good and acceptable, and perfect will of God" (Romans 12:1–2).

Paul stressed that the good news of Jesus Christ is more than facts to be believed in; it is a life to be lived. He devoted the latter chapters of Romans to many practical and vital aspects of living for God. A few examples illustrate why the esteemed theologian Frederick Godet called this book "the cathedral of Christianity":

- Let love be without hypocrisy. Abhor what is evil. Cling to what is good.
- Bless those who persecute you; bless and do not curse.

- Be of the same mind toward one another. Do not set your mind on high things, but associate with the humble. Do not be wise in your own opinion.
- Repay no one evil for evil.
- If your enemy is hungry, feed him; if he is thirsty, give him a drink; For in so doing you will heap coals of fire on his head.
- Do not be overcome by evil, but overcome evil with good.
- Owe no one anything except to love one another.
- Love does no harm to a neighbor; therefore, love is the fulfillment of the law.
- Put on the Lord Jesus Christ, and make no provision for the flesh to fulfill its lusts.

"None of us lives to himself, and no one dies to himself," Paul continued. "For if we live, we live to the Lord, and if we die, we die to the Lord. Therefore, whether we live or die, we are the Lord's" (Romans 14:7–8).

By the time he wrote the letter that became known as his greatest work, Paul was convinced that to live is Christ and to die is gain. He preached that we (Christians) are to die to sin, to not allow sin to have dominion over our lives, but to come alive in Jesus Christ and become "slaves to righteousness."

"Who shall separate us from the love of Christ?" he asked. "Shall tribulation, or distress, or persecution, or famine, or nakedness, or peril or sword? As it is written, 'For your sakes we are killed all day long; we are accounted as sheep for the slaughter.' Yet in all these things we are more than conquerors through Him who loved us. For I am persuaded that neither death nor life, nor angels now principalities, nor powers, nor things present nor things to come, nor height nor depth, nor any other created thing, shall be able to separate us from the love of God which is in Christ Jesus our Lord" (Romans 8:35–39).

In praise of the Roman Christians, Paul wrote, "I thank my God through Jesus Christ for you all, that your faith is spoken of throughout the whole world. For God is my witness, whom I serve with my spirit in the gospel of His Son, that without ceasing I make mention of you always in my prayers, making request if, by some means, now at last I may find a way in the will of God to come to you."

He closed with thanks to people who had helped him in ministry, including Priscilla and Aquila, "my fellow workers in Christ Jesus, who risked their own necks for my life, to whom not only I give thanks, but also all the churches of the Gentiles" (Romans 16:4).

"I want you to be wise in what is good and simple concerning evil," Paul concluded. "And the God of peace will crush Satan under your feet shortly. The grace of our Lord Jesus Christ be with you. Amen."

The Holy Spirit's living presence in the hearts of the first missionaries for Jesus Christ is the greatest power that can take charge of my life; it can give me a heart of real compassion and realistic hope for eternal life beginning now. The Spirit within me is the empowering presence of Almighty God, Who comforts and guides me (and all believers) through sunny days and troubled times.

EPILOGUE

Timeless Message of Power from a Timeless God

Passion, energy, and inspiration marked the renowned ministries of two brothers: John Wesley, the preacher, and Charles Wesley, the prolific hymn writer, in eighteenth-century England, Ireland, and Georgia in the American colonies. Traveling most often by horseback, John preached two to three times a day, and Charles composed hymns as they rode along. They are credited with leading evangelical movements that resulted in the conversion of more than a million people. The Methodist movement they organized in the Church of England evolved into the international Methodist Church.

By the numbers, the Wesley brothers were impressive soul-winners for Christ, but following a failed missionary venture to Savannah, Georgia, both suffered a siege of doubt and insecurity about their faith.

Despite their impressive theological education at Christ Church, Oxford University, and excellent skills in ministry, both Charles and John sensed a major shortcoming in their relationship with Him. They began to pray for a greater inner presence of God after befriending a group of Moravian Christians (German Protestants) in October 1735. The friendship took root aboard ship while sailing from Gravesend in Kent to Savannah. At the time, John was thirty-two and Charles a few years younger.

As the brothers recalled, their lives were severely threatened when their sailing ship, the *Simmonds*, was battered by a massive storm. In the midst of terrorizing wind, the mast of the ship was broken off, and the mainsail was split, and while the English passengers screamed in panic, the Moravians calmly sang hymns, prayed, and comforted others. The Moravians' behavior was in keeping with their belief that Christians have an assurance of faith experienced as love, peace, and joy. They continued to influence John and Charles as they began what they intended to be a successful missionary work in the young colony founded by General James Oglethorpe.

General Oglethorpe had called for John Wesley to become chaplain of the newly formed Savannah parish, and Charles would serve as Oglethorpe's secretary. But through unfortunate circumstances, their efforts were unsuccessful, and the brothers returned to England, depressed and defeated. At this point, longing for a stronger and more vibrant faith, they received counsel from a Moravian minister, Peter Boehler.

For Charles, the answer to his prayers occurred on May 21, 1738, while he was seriously ill with pleurisy. He had a personal encounter with the Holy Spirit and found himself at peace with God. Three days later, John also received the blessing of the Holy Spirit in his heart at a Moravian meeting in Aldersgate Street, London, where he heard a reading of Luther's preface to the Epistle to the Romans.

"I felt my heart strangely warmed," John wrote after that meeting, which he called his Aldersgate experience. The missionary work of John and Charles was revolutionized. As with the original disciples of Christ, they would be led by that indwelling Holy Spirit for the rest of their lives.

John believed he was commissioned by God to bring about revival in the church. No opposition, persecution, or obstacles could prevail against the divine urgency and authority of this commission. Following the example set by George Whitefield, his Oxford colleague and evangelist who led the Great Awakening in North America, Wesley began preaching in open fields and appointed lay ministers to expand the church. At the same time, Charles composed more than sixty-five hundred hymns, which continue to make an inspiring impact on people who sing them.

The sanctifying work of the Holy Spirit became the major theme of John's preaching, as he urged men and women to become living portraits of Jesus Christ. In his sermon, "On the Holy Spirit," he said the Spirit moves us toward the completed state (holiness) that will be realized in eternity.

"The gift of the Holy Spirit looks full to the resurrection, for then is the life of God completed in us," he said. He also preached that believers in Christ can know whether they are children of God through the inner testimony of the Holy Spirit, and that this assurance is experienced as an inward peace, joy, love, and delight.

John and Charles Wesley are among a great line of Christian evangelists, who have stepped forward time after time in the twenty-one centuries since the resurrection of Christ, to remind men and women that the gifts of the Holy Spirit did not end after the Age of the Apostles. They believed the gifts of the Spirit were important and active in the eighteenth-century Evangelical Revival and continue to be an expected part of the life of faith anywhere, anytime.

As the apostle Peter proclaimed on the day of Pentecost a little over two thousand years ago, "The promise is for you and your children and for all who are far off—for all whom the Lord our God will call." Peter's forecast indicated no time limit on God's blessing of believers with the power of the Holy Spirit. On the day of Pentecost, shortly after Christ returned to heaven in an ascension witnessed by the apostles, nothing less could soothe the deeply wounded souls of people who saw some part of His cruel execution.

In today's world of sharply conflicting ideologies, hate speech, moral decay, corporate and business corruption, abortions on demand, and violent threats against people of faith, nothing exceeds the Holy Spirit's ability to heal the human heart and to bring about peaceful resolutions, no matter how huge or complicated the problem.

The Holy Spirit is not a temporal concept of ancient scripture. He is the timeless living Spirit of God the Father, constantly at the sides and in the hearts of believers. He is the Spirit Who raised Jesus Christ from death to life and assures everlasting life to every person who believes He is the Son of God.

> When He is in you, He cannot be separated from you. In God's scheme of things, a person blessed in this magnificent way possesses a guiding, comforting, strengthening inner presence that has no equal.

HUMAN HOPES RISE WITH THE RISEN CHRIST

A seventeen-foot-long steel crossbeam, found amid the blasted wreckage of the World Trade Center shortly after the terrorist attacks on September 11, 2001, became a symbol of hope to thousands of people who lost relatives and friends in the disaster. A grief-exhausted Christian excavator named Frank Silechhia found the cross in the rubble of twisted steel and concrete, and a Franciscan priest named Father Brian Jordan blessed it among other remains at Ground Zero. (Photo source: Wikipedia)

It must have been lonely on that cross,
lonelier still in the tomb of cold, cold rock.
Lonelier than the snowy peaks of Gibraltar,
standing solid in the icy winds of winter.

The Man on the cross, the Man in the grave
had to have known his disciples were hiding away,
away from the mob that suffocated his last breath,
away from the place of unthinkable pain and death.

How could they let it be known at that terrible time
they had chosen to leave ordinary life behind,
to follow the man who claimed to be the Son of God,
in bold opposition to the teachings at synagogue?

He had been killed, the disciples knew and were in fear
that life was at risk for followers of this preacher.
They might as well run on and on, too afraid to stay,
for hopes stirred by the Man of grace had been swept away.
The disciples were gripped in grief, despair, and torment
How could the Son of God lose his life to angry men?
Their reason for hope in eternal life was now voiceless
in that grave, as inert as hard rock forever silent.

Lives of bitter memory and disappointment seemed certain,
until three days after burial, when the unthinkable happened.
Jesus cast off his grave clothes, left them neatly folded there
and walked into the garden to breathe the brisk morning air.

A woman saw Him in the rising light and heard Him call her Mary,
but He left quickly to seek out the disciples locked in sanctuary.
Unannounced, He walked through the door as if it were not there
to greet His friends, staring wide-eyed, as if at a specter.

Jesus had risen, and nothing on earth would be the same ever after.
Soon He was back in full form, talking, fishing, sharing the fresh fish,
and with bold conviction teaching the undying love of God the Father.

The blood-stained cross and the tomb faded into the dustbin of history,
as the resurrected Son of God preached until His return to heaven,
filling broken hearts with His promise for life that will have no end.
The disciples, no longer in terror and buoyed by the Spirit within,
took the resurrection story to distant places they had never been.
It was the miracle of miracles of changed men who changed the world.

BIBLIOGRAPHY

Bibles

The Holy Bible, New King James Version. Thomas Nelson Inc., 1982.

The Thompson Chain-Reference Bible, King James Version, Fifth Improved Edition. Indianapolis: B. B. Kirkbride Bible Co., 1988.

NIV Cultural Backgrounds Study Bible. Zondervan, 2016.

Books

Eldredge, John. *Beautiful Outlaw*. New York: FaithWorks, Hatchett Book Group, 2011.

Foxe, John. *Foxe's Book of Martyrs*. Hendrickson Publishers, 2006.

Graham, Billy. *The Journey: How to Live by Faith in an Uncertain World*. Nashville: W. Publishing Group, a division of Thomas Nelson Inc., 2006.

Graham, Billy. *The Holy Spirit*. Waco, TX: Word Books, 1978.

Lewis, C. S. *Mere Christianity*. New York: Touchstone Books, Simon & Schuster, 1996.

McBirnie, William Steuart. *The Search for the Twelve Apostles.* Wheaton, IL: Living Books, Tyndale House Publishers Inc.

McDowell, Josh, and Sean McDowell. *More Than a Carpenter.* Tyndale House Publishers Inc., 1977, 2005, 2009.

Metzger, Bruce M., and Michael Coogan, editors. *Oxford Guide to the Bible.* Oxford, UK, and New York: Oxford University Press, 1993.

Platt, David. *Radical: Taking Back Your Faith from the American Dream.* Colorado Springs: Multnomah Books, 2010.

Pollock, John. *The Apostle: A Life of Paul.* Colorado Springs: David C. Cook, 2012.

Torrey, R. A., *The Person and Work of the Holy Spirit.* Zondervan Publishing House, 1974.

Deep-field view of space from NASA/ESA Hubble Space Telescope, labeled "Mystic Mountain."

Old Testament prophet Jeramiah speaks of creation: "He has made the earth by His power, He has established the world by His wisdom, and He has stretched out the heavens at His discretion" (Jeremiah 10:12).